Home-Cooked Weeknight Dinners
Are Possible with Fast, Flavorful Recipes!

DOESN'T it seem like life just keeps getting busier? Work, school, errands…the list goes on and on. Squeezing in time for eating meals is difficult, let alone the time to cook them. Drive-thru and take-out seem like good choices because they're speedy, but in the long run, they're not satisfying.

This book will take a big load off your shoulders because it puts an end to the "What's for Dinner" dilemma—with wholesome, home-cooked dinners in a snap.

Taste of Home's Weeknight Cooking Made Easy 2006 is packed with 304 mouth-watering recipes that let you get a tasty, homemade dinner on the table in mere minutes. Here's what sets this one-of-a-kind cookbook apart from all others:

• **Ideal ingredients.** *Taste of Home's Weeknight Cooking Made Easy 2006* provides a balance of fresh and convenience foods to offer from-scratch goodness. Plus, the recipes use a *reasonable number* of everyday ingredients. (In fact, 70 recipes use 5 ingredients or fewer!)

• **Focus on main dishes.** Entrees are the meat and potatoes to meal planning. You'll find 236 main dishes, featuring beef, ground beef, chicken, turkey, pork and seafood in addition to meatless entree ideas.

• **Speed is key.** This book offers 283 recipes that go from start to finish in less than 30 minutes. (And 80 of those recipes can be ready in under 15 minutes!)

• **Beautiful photos.** We know you're more likely to try recipes with a picture. So we've included a gorgeous, color photo of *each and every recipe!*

• **Prep and cooking times.** The preparation and cooking times for each dish are prominently displayed, making it easy to find recipes that fit your schedule.

• **Hundreds of helpful hints.** Each recipe features at least one timely tip, such as tricks that reduce preparation time, facts for buying and storing foods, substitution secrets and ideas for speedy side dishes.

• **Easy on the eyes.** *Taste of Home's Weeknight Cooking Made Easy 2006* is so easy to read because there is only one recipe on a page.

• **Recipe list by chapter.** Quickly browse through the recipes in each chapter without turning a page! Just go to the beginning of each chapter for the list of recipes.

With *Taste of Home's Weeknight Cooking Made Easy 2006*, offering your family a wholesome meal night after night couldn't be easier!

Weeknight Cooking Made Easy 2006

Taste of Home Books
©2006 Reiman Media Group, Inc.
5400 S. 60th St., Greendale WI 53129
International Standard Book Number: 0-89821-502-1
International Standard Serial Number: 1555-0400
All rights reserved.
Printed in U.S.A.

For additional copies of this book, write *Taste of Home* Books, P.O. Box 908, Greendale WI 53129. Or to order by credit card, call toll-free 1-800/344-2560 or visit our Web site at **www.reimanpub.com**.

PICTURED ON THE COVER:
Chicken with Pears and Squash (p. 110)

Executive Editor, Books: Heidi Reuter Lloyd

Project Editor: Julie Schnittka

Senior Layout Designer: Julie Wagner

Associate Layout Designer: Catherine Fletcher

Associate Project Designer: Kevin Kossow

Editorial Assistant: Barb Czysz

Proofreaders: Linne Bruskewitz, Jean Steiner

Taste of Home Test Kitchens

Food Editor: Janaan Cunningham

Associate Food Editors: Diane Werner RD, Coleen Martin

Assistant Food Editor: Karen Scales

Senior Recipe Editor: Sue A. Jurack

Recipe Editor: Mary King

Test Kitchen Home Economists: Tina Johnson, Ann Liebergen, Annie Rose, Pat Schmeling, Wendy Stenman, Amy Thieding, Peggy Woodword RD

Test Kitchen Assistants: Rita Krajcir, Kris Lehman, Sue Megonigle, Megan Taylor

Taste of Home Photo Studio

Senior Food Photographer: Rob Hagen

Food Photograpers: Dan Roberts, Jim Wieland

Associate Food Photographer: Lori Foy

Set Stylists: Julie Ferron, Stephanie Marchese, Sue Myers, Jennifer Bradley Vent

Assistant Set Stylist: Melissa Haberman

Senior Food Stylist: Joylyn Trickel

Food Stylist: Sarah Thompson

Photo Studio Coordinator: Suzanne Kern

Reiman Media Group, Inc.

Creative Director: Ardyth Cope

Senior Vice President, Editor in Chief: Catherine Cassidy

President: Barbara Newton

Founder: Roy Reiman

Easy Weekday Menus

Whether you're eating on the run or are actually able to enjoy a sit-down dinner, here are complete meal suggestions using both recipes from *Weeknight Cooking Made Easy* and purchased items.

After-Soccer Supper

Serves 6 to 8

Flip the switch and forget it when assembling this hearty roast in the morning. Then when you and the kids head in the door after school, work and soccer, the main course is ready and waiting!

Slow-Cooked Rump Roast (p. 79)
Romaine with Oranges and Almonds (p. 260)
Swiss Onion Crescents (p. 285)
Assorted purchased cookies

Grilled Goodies

Serves 4 to 6

Here's a great way to relax on a summer night. Escape the heat of the kitchen by cooking the main course, side dish and even dessert on the grill! Round out the meal with fresh bread.

Cranberry Turkey Cutlets (p. 134)
Zesty Vegetable Skewers (p. 289)
Fresh bread or rolls
Chocolate Dessert Wraps (p. 297)

Soup & Sandwich Supper

Serves 5

Nothing could be simpler to make on a busy weeknight than sandwiches and soup. Your family will be fans of these perfect partners, and you'll favor the fast preparation!

The Ultimate Grilled Cheese (p. 202)
Salsa Chili (p. 47)
Potato or corn chips
Cookie Ice Cream Sandwiches (p. 306)

Pizza Night

Serves 10 to 12

After watching the football game on Friday, invite friends over for a pizza party featuring an assortment of quick-to-fix, savory pies. Enlist guests to help assemble them for a fun-filled night!

French Bread Pizza (p. 40)
Ham 'n' Broccoli Pizza (p. 168)
Tomato Pizza Bread (p. 274)
Tossed salad
Bakery brownies

Special Celebration

Serves 4

Special occasions don't wait for the weekend. Celebrate a job promotion, stellar report card or sporting achievement with this easy, yet elegant menu.

Pork Tenderloin Diane (p. 185)
Zesty Sugar Snap Peas (p. 275)
Rice pilaf
Chocolate Chip Mousse (p. 294)

Down-Home Dinner

Serves 4

Comfort foods shouldn't only appear on your Sunday dinner table. Treat your family to these classics today.

Quick Comforting Chicken (p. 92)
Apple Spinach Salad (p. 283)
Easy Boston Cream Cake (p. 323)

From-the-Sea Fare

Serves 4

Catch your family's attention at the dinner table when presenting this seafood supper. Then get ready to net a host of compliments!

Nut-Crusted Fried Fish (p. 239)
Colorful Couscous (p. 268)
Puffed Apple Pastries (p. 304)

Italian Cuisine

Serves 4

There's no need to venture out to a restaurant when you can create a taste of Little Italy in your own kitchen.

Parmesan Chicken (p. 90)
Purchased breadsticks
Italian Vegetable Saute (p. 258)
Smooth Vanilla Shakes (p. 316)

Make It Mexican!

Serves 6

When your family craves south-of-the-border cuisine, rely on zesty fajitas and a box of Spanish rice. Then cool your palate with a refreshing dessert.

Steak Fajitas (p. 78)
Spanish rice
Butterscotch Parfaits (p. 314)

Orient Express

Serves 6

When you have a hankering for Asian cooking, skip picking up takeout and make a meal at home.

Stir-Fried Pork Soup (p. 193)
Turkey Stir-Fry (p. 135)
Egg rolls
Fortune cookies

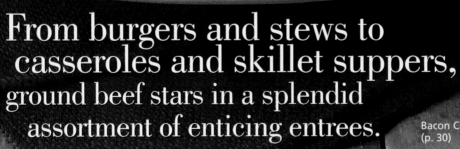

From burgers and stews to casseroles and skillet suppers, ground beef stars in a splendid assortment of enticing entrees.

Bacon Cheeseburger Pasta (p. 30)

Speedy Ground Beef

All-American Hamburgers (p. 8)

All-American Hamburgers

Prep/Total Time: 20 min.

2 tablespoons diced onion

2 tablespoons chili sauce

2 teaspoons Worcestershire sauce

2 teaspoons prepared mustard

1 pound ground beef

4 slices American *or* cheddar cheese, halved diagonally

2 slices Swiss cheese, halved diagonally

4 hamburger buns, split and toasted

Lettuce leaves, sliced tomato and onion, cooked bacon, ketchup and mustard, optional

In a bowl, combine the first four ingredients. Crumble beef over mixture and mix well. Shape into four patties. Grill, covered, over medium heat for 6 minutes on each side or until meat is no longer pink.

During the last minute of cooking, top each patty with two triangles of American cheese and one triangle of Swiss cheese. Serve on buns with lettuce, tomato, onion, bacon, ketchup and mustard if desired.

Yield: 4 servings.

Burger Bar

When serving burgers, set out a platter loaded with assorted condiments and toppings.

Traditional additions include lettuce, tomato and onion slices, cheese, pickles, cooked bacon strips, ketchup and mustard.

But don't forget mayonnaise, butter, salsa, pickled jalapeno slices and even guacamole.

Hot offerings could include sauteed mushrooms, warmed process cheese sauce or a can of heated chili.

Chili Nacho Supper

Prep/Total Time: 20 min.

2-1/2	pounds ground beef
3	cans (15 ounces *each*) tomato sauce
2	cans (16 ounces *each*) pinto beans, rinsed and drained
1	can (10 ounces) diced tomatoes and green chilies, undrained
2	envelopes chili seasoning
2	pounds process American cheese, cubed
1	cup heavy whipping cream
2	packages (16 ounces *each*) corn chips

Sour cream

In a Dutch oven, cook the beef over medium heat until no longer pink; drain. Add tomato sauce, beans, tomatoes and chili seasoning; heat through. Add cheese and cream; cook until the cheese is melted. Serve over chips. Top with sour cream.

Yield: 14-16 servings.

Chip Choices

Corn chips come in a variety of sizes. Buy the larger ones for easier scooping.

You can also replace the corn chips with regular and flavored tortilla chips or multigrain chips.

Party Snack

Chili Nacho Supper would also make great party fare. Prepare as directed; transfer to a slow cooker and heat on low throughout the party. Serve chips and sour cream on the side.

Barbecued Onion Meat Loaves

Prep/Total Time: 25 min.

  1 egg, beaten
1/3 cup milk
  2 tablespoons plus 1/4 cup
     barbecue sauce, *divided*
1/2 cup crushed stuffing
  1 tablespoon onion soup mix
1-1/4 pounds ground beef

In a bowl, combine the egg, milk, 2 tablespoons barbecue sauce, stuffing and onion soup mix. Crumble beef over mixture and mix well. Shape into five loaves; arrange around the edge of a microwave-safe dish.

Microwave, uncovered, on high for 6-7 minutes or until a meat thermometer reads 160°. Cover and let stand for 5-10 minutes. Top with the remaining barbecue sauce.

Editor's Note: This recipe was tested in an 850-watt microwave.

Yield: 5 servings.

Keep Beef Handy

Ground beef is often sold in 3-pound packages. Use 1-1/4 pounds in these Barbecued Onion Meat Loaves.

Then freeze 3/4 pound to make a batch of Southwestern Spaghetti on the opposite page.

The remaining pound of ground beef can be used in a number of other recipes in this chapter.

Or freeze two 1/2-pound packages to make both Green Chili Burritos (p. 36) and French Bread Pizza (p. 40).

Southwestern Spaghetti

Prep/Total Time: 30 min.

3/4	pound ground beef
2-1/4	cups water
1	can (15 ounces) tomato sauce
2	teaspoons chili powder
1/2	teaspoon garlic powder
1/2	teaspoon salt
1/2	teaspoon ground cumin
1	package (7 ounces) thin spaghetti, broken into thirds
6	small zucchini (about 1 pound), cut into chunks
1/2	cup shredded cheddar cheese

In a large skillet, cook beef over medium heat until no longer pink; drain. Remove beef and keep warm. In the same skillet, combine the water, tomato sauce, chili powder, garlic powder, salt and cumin; bring to a boil. Stir in spaghetti; return to a boil. Boil for 6 minutes.

Add the zucchini. Cook 4-5 minutes longer or until spaghetti and zucchini are tender, stirring several times. Stir in the beef; sprinkle with cheese. Serve immediately.

Yield: 5 servings.

A Course in Cumin

During the Middle Ages, it was believed a bride and groom were guaranteed a happy life if they carried cumin seed during the ceremony.

Ground cumin must be kept in an airtight container to retain its strong flavor.

Use cumin with restraint in your cooking because it can be overpowering.

Beef 'n' Biscuit Bake

Prep/Total Time: 30 min.

1 pound ground beef
1 can (16 ounces) kidney beans, rinsed and drained
1 can (15-1/4 ounces) whole kernel corn, drained
1 can (10-3/4 ounces) condensed tomato soup, undiluted
1/4 cup milk
2 tablespoons minced onion
1/2 teaspoon chili powder
1/4 teaspoon salt
1 cup cubed process cheese (Velveeta)
1 tube (12 ounces) refrigerated biscuits
2 to 3 tablespoons butter, melted
1/3 cup yellow cornmeal

In a saucepan over medium heat, cook beef over medium heat until no longer pink; drain. Add beans, corn, soup, milk, onion, chili powder and salt; bring to a boil. Remove from the heat; stir in cheese until melted. Spoon into a greased 2-1/2-qt. baking dish. Bake, uncovered, at 375° for 10 minutes.

Meanwhile, brush all sides of biscuits with butter; roll in cornmeal. Place on top of bubbling meat mixture. Return to the oven for 10-12 minutes or until biscuits are lightly browned and cooked through.

Yield: 6-8 servings.

Simple Substitution

For a little more zest, replace the regular process cheese with a mild or hot Mexican variety.

Speedy Salad

Pick up a prepackaged salad kit to serve alongside Beef 'n' Biscuit Bake.

With mouth-watering options like Caesar, Romano cheese, ranch and Asian, you're sure to find something to suit your family's taste.

Tater Tot Taco Salad

Prep/Total Time: 30 min.

    4   cups frozen miniature Tater Tots
    1   pound ground beef
  1/4   cup taco seasoning
    1   cup (4 ounces) shredded cheddar cheese
  1/2   cup sliced ripe *or* stuffed olives
    2   cups shredded lettuce
  1/4   cup taco sauce
  1/2   cup sour cream

Bake Tater Tots according to package directions. Meanwhile, in a large skillet, cook beef over medium heat until no longer pink; drain. Stir in taco seasoning. Divide Tater Tots between four serving plates or bowls. Top with taco mixture, cheese, olives, lettuce, taco sauce and sour cream.

Yield: 4 servings.

Serving Suggestion

For added nutrition, top this salad with assorted fresh vegetables, like tomato, cucumber, bell peppers, carrots and broccoli.

Try Other Taters

This deliciously different salad would be tasty with any frozen potato, including French fries, steak fries, shoestrings, waffle fries, hash browns and roasted potatoes.

Colorful Stuffed Peppers

Prep/Total Time: 30 min.

- 1 pound ground beef
- 2 cups salsa
- 1 cup frozen corn
- 1/4 cup water
- 3/4 teaspoon ground cumin
- 3/4 teaspoon dried oregano
- 1 teaspoon salt
- 1/2 teaspoon pepper
- 1/2 cup uncooked instant rice
- 1 cup (4 ounces) shredded cheddar cheese, *divided*
- 4 medium green peppers, halved lengthwise

Sliced canned jalapeno peppers, optional

Crumble beef into a 2-qt. microwave-safe dish. Cover and microwave on high for 2 minutes; stir. Cook on high 1-2 minutes longer or until the meat is no longer pink; drain. Stir in the salsa, corn, water, cumin, oregano, salt and pepper.

Cover and microwave on high for 3 minutes or until mixture bubbles around the edges. Stir in rice and 1/2 cup cheese. Cover and let stand for 5 minutes; stir. Spoon 1/2 cup into each pepper half. Place on a 12-in. round microwave-safe plate.

Cover loosely and cook on high for 8-10 minutes or until peppers are tender, rotating a half turn once. Cover and let stand for 4 minutes. Sprinkle with remaining cheese; top with jalapenos if desired.

Editor's Note: This recipe was tested in an 850-watt microwave.

Yield: 4 servings.

Pepper Pointers

Look for green peppers that are firm, glossy and brightly colored.

Store peppers in your refrigerator's crisper drawer for up to 1 week. Wash just before using.

Ground Beef Stroganoff

Prep/Total Time: 30 min.

1 pound ground beef
1/2 cup chopped onion
2 tablespoons butter
1/2 cup sliced fresh mushrooms
2 tablespoons all-purpose flour
2 garlic cloves, minced
1/2 teaspoon salt
1/4 teaspoon pepper
1/4 cup chili sauce
1/2 teaspoon Worcestershire sauce
2/3 cup sour cream
Hot cooked noodles

In a skillet, cook beef and onion in butter over medium heat until meat is no longer pink. Stir in mushrooms, flour, garlic, salt and pepper. Cook and stir for 5 minutes. Add chili sauce and Worcestershire sauce. Reduce heat; cook, uncovered, for 10 minutes. Stir in sour cream just before serving; heat through (do not boil). Serve over noodles.

Yield: 4 servings.

Stroganoff Story

Beef Stroganoff was created by the Stroganov family chef for a cooking competition in the 1890s.

Traditional Stroganoff calls for beef cubes. This version uses quick-cooking ground beef with equally good results.

Serving Suggestion

Stroganoff is traditionally served over noodles. But try it with rice and mashed potatoes. Or look for a package of dried spaetzle noodles at the store.

Chili Stew

Prep/Total Time: 30 min.

- 1 pound ground beef
- 1 medium onion, chopped
- 1 small green pepper, chopped
- 2 cans (15-1/2 ounces *each*) hot chili beans
- 1 can (16 ounces) kidney beans, rinsed and drained
- 1 can (15-1/4 ounces) whole kernel corn, drained
- 1 can (14-1/2 ounces) diced tomatoes with garlic and onion
- 1 can (8 ounces) tomato sauce
- 1 can (4 ounces) chopped green chilies
- 2 tablespoons chili powder
- 1/2 teaspoon salt

In a Dutch oven or large saucepan, cook the beef, onion and green pepper over medium heat until meat is no longer pink; drain. Stir in remaining ingredients. Bring to a boil. Reduce heat; simmer, uncovered, for 15 minutes, stirring occasionally.

Yield: 10 servings.

Bread Bowls

Hard rolls (about 4-1/2 inches) make quick and easy bread bowls for Chili Stew.

Cut the top fourth off of each roll; carefully hollow out bottom, leaving a 1-1/2-in. shell. Cube the removed bread. Spoon Chili Stew into bread bowls. Serve with cubed bread for dipping.

Blue Plate Beef Patties

Prep/Total Time: 20 min.

> 1 egg
> 2 green onions with tops, sliced
> 1/4 cup seasoned bread crumbs
> 1 tablespoon prepared mustard
> 1-1/2 pounds ground beef
> 1 jar (12 ounces) beef gravy
> 1/2 cup water
> 2 to 3 teaspoons prepared horseradish
> 1/2 pound fresh mushrooms, sliced

In a bowl, beat the egg; stir in onions, bread crumbs and mustard. Add beef and mix well. Shape into four 1/2-in.-thick patties. In an ungreased skillet, cook patties for 4-5 minutes on each side or until meat is no longer pink; drain.

In a small bowl, combine gravy, water and horseradish; add mushrooms. Pour over patties. Cook, uncovered, for 5 minutes or until mushrooms are tender and heated through.

Yield: 4 servings.

Select Fresh 'Shrooms'

For faster preparation, pick up an 8-ounce package of sliced mushrooms instead of buying whole mushrooms and slicing them yourself.

Freezer Fact

Double the recipe for Blue Plate Beef Patties. Freeze half in a heavy-duty plastic container. Reheat when you need dinner in a dash.

Busy Day Dinner

Prep/Total Time: 30 min.

1 pound ground beef
1/4 cup chopped onion
3/4 teaspoon salt
1/4 teaspoon pepper
Dash garlic powder
1 can (19 ounces) ready-to-serve chunky beef vegetable soup
4 ounces spaghetti, cooked and drained
1 cup (4 ounces) shredded cheddar cheese
Minced fresh parsley, optional

In a skillet, cook beef and onion over medium heat until meat is no longer pink; drain. Stir in salt, pepper and garlic powder. Transfer to a greased 2-qt. baking dish. Pour soup over meat mixture. Top with spaghetti and cheese. Bake, uncovered, at 350° for 15-20 minutes or until heated through. Sprinkle with parsley if desired.

Yield: 4-6 servings.

Preparation Pointer

You can make the spaghetti for this recipe the night before. Cook as directed; drain well. Place in a resealable plastic bag and refrigerate.

The next day, place the spaghetti on top of the meat mixture, sprinkle with the cheese and bake as directed.

Slow-Cooker Enchiladas

Prep: 30 min.   **Cook:** 5 hours

1   pound ground beef
1   cup chopped onion
1/2   cup chopped green pepper
1   can (16 ounces) pinto *or* kidney beans, rinsed and drained
1   can (15 ounces) black beans, rinsed and drained
1   can (10 ounces) diced tomatoes and green chilies, undrained
1/3   cup water
1   teaspoon chili powder
1/2   teaspoon ground cumin
1/2   teaspoon salt
1/4   teaspoon pepper
1   cup (4 ounces) shredded sharp cheddar cheese
1   cup (4 ounces) shredded Monterey Jack cheese
6   flour tortillas (6 inches)

In a skillet, cook beef, onion and green pepper until beef is browned and vegetables are tender; drain. Add the next eight ingredients; bring to a boil. Reduce heat; cover and simmer for 10 minutes. Combine the cheeses.

In a 5-qt. slow cooker, layer about 3/4 cup beef mixture, one tortilla and about 1/3 cup cheese. Repeat layers. Cover and cook on low for 5-7 hours or until heated through.

Yield: 4 servings.

Timely Tip

Not looking forward to the messy cleanup after using your slow cooker? Pick up a package of nylon slow cooker liners. (You'll find them in the same aisle as plastic wrap and aluminum foil.)

Simply place a liner in your slow cooker and add the ingredients. When done cooking, remove the food, let the liner cool and toss!

Corn Bread Hamburger Pie

Prep/Total Time: 30 min.

1   pound ground beef
1   medium onion, chopped
1   medium green pepper, chopped
1   can (10-3/4 ounces) condensed tomato soup, undiluted
1/4   cup salsa
2   tablespoons ketchup
1   tablespoon steak sauce, optional
1   package (8-1/2 ounces) corn bread/muffin mix
Minced fresh parsley, optional

In a 10-in. ovenproof skillet, cook the beef, onion and green pepper over medium heat until meat is no longer pink; drain. Stir in the soup, salsa, ketchup and steak sauce if desired.

Prepare corn bread batter according to package directions; let stand for 2 minutes. Spoon over beef mixture. Bake at 400° for 15 minutes or until lightly browned. Sprinkle with parsley if desired.

Yield: 4-6 servings.

Keep Cooked Beef Handy

When you have time, cook a few pounds of ground beef. Add chopped onion, chopped green pepper and minced garlic if you like. Drain; let cool.

Freeze in heavy-duty plastic bags or plastic containers. One pound of ground beef yields 2-1/2 to 3 cups (loosely packed). Four pounds equals 10 to 12 cups.

Pull out a package and thaw whenever a recipe calls for cooked ground beef.

Beefy Bacon Pizza

Prep/Total Time: 20 min.

1/2 pound ground beef
1 small onion, chopped
1 prebaked Italian bread shell crust (1 pound)
1 can (8 ounces) pizza sauce
6 bacon strips, cooked and crumbled
20 dill pickle coin slices
2 cups (8 ounces) shredded mozzarella cheese
2 cups (8 ounces) shredded cheddar cheese
1 teaspoon pizza *or* Italian seasoning

In a skillet, cook beef and onion over medium heat until meat is no longer pink; drain and set aside. Place crust on an ungreased 12-in. pizza pan. Spread with pizza sauce. Top with beef mixture, bacon, pickles and cheeses. Sprinkle with pizza seasoning. Bake at 450° for 8-10 minutes or until cheese is melted.

Yield: 8 slices.

Making Bacon

No one can resist the smell of bacon cooking. But the time it takes (including cleanup time) is something folks can't always afford.

Look for boxes of ready-to-serve bacon near the packaged deli meats. Remove only as many strips as needed. For Beefy Bacon Pizza, there isn't even any need to heat it!

Chuck Wagon Burgers

Prep/Total Time: 25 min.

2 pounds ground beef
1 envelope onion soup mix
1/2 cup water
1 tube (16.3 ounces) large refrigerated biscuits
1/8 teaspoon seasoned salt

In a bowl, combine the beef, soup mix and water; mix well. Shape into eight 3/4-in.-thick patties. Grill, uncovered, or broil 4 in. from the heat for 5-6 minutes on each side or until meat is no longer pink.

Meanwhile, place biscuits on an ungreased baking sheet; sprinkle with seasoned salt. Bake at 375° for 12-14 minutes or until golden brown. Split; top each biscuit with a hamburger.

Yield: 8 servings.

Best Baked Beans

Baked beans add a Southwestern flair to a dinner featuring Chuck Wagon Burgers.

In a large saucepan, combine one 28-oz. can baked beans, one 14-1/2-oz. can diced tomatoes with mild green chilies and one 15-1/4-oz. can whole kernel corn.

Cook over medium-high heat until heated through.

Simple Taco Soup

Prep/Total Time: 25 min.

 2 pounds ground beef
 1 envelope taco seasoning mix
1-1/2 cups water
 1 can (15-3/4 ounces) mild chili beans
 1 can (15-1/4 ounces) whole kernel corn, drained
 1 can (15 ounces) pinto beans, rinsed and drained
 1 can (14-1/2 ounces) stewed tomatoes
 1 can (10 ounces) diced tomato with green chilies
 1 can (4 ounces) chopped green chilies, optional
 1 envelope ranch salad dressing mix

In a Dutch oven or large kettle, cook beef over medium heat until no longer pink; drain. Add taco seasoning and mix well. Stir in remaining ingredients. Simmer, uncovered, for 15 minutes or until heated through, stirring occasionally.

Yield: 6-8 servings (about 2 quarts).

Savory Crescents

Dress up one 8-oz. package of refrigerated crescent rolls and serve with this soup.

Separate the dough into eight triangles. Sprinkle with 4 teaspoons grated Parmesan cheese and 3/4 teaspoon garlic powder. Roll up dough, starting from the wide end. Place point side down on a greased baking sheet. Brush with one beaten egg; sprinkle with 1 teaspoon sesame seeds.

Bake at 375° for 11-13 minutes or until golden.

Dinner in a Bag

Prep: 5 min.   **Cook:** 25 min.

1   pound ground beef
2   cans (14-1/2 ounces *each*)
    stewed tomatoes
1/4   cup dried minced onion
1   teaspoon salt
1   teaspoon chili powder
1/4   to 1/2 teaspoon pepper
1/4   teaspoon sugar
1   cup uncooked elbow
    macaroni

In a skillet, cook beef over medium heat until no longer pink; drain. Add tomatoes and seasonings; bring to a boil. Reduce heat and simmer for 5 minutes. Stir in macaroni; cover and simmer for 15 minutes. Uncover; simmer until macaroni is tender and sauce is thickened.

Yield: 4 servings.

Pantry Pleaser

Give dinner a head start by creating this "pantry kit."

Measure the dry macaroni and mixture of spices for Dinner in a Bag; place in separate plastic bags. Store them in a paper bag along with the canned stewed tomatoes.

At dinnertime, just cook the ground beef and soon dinner is simmering!

Meatball Shish Kabobs

Prep/Total Time: 30 min.

     1   package (16 ounces) frozen fully cooked
         meatballs, thawed (about 30 meatballs)
     2   medium zucchini, cut into 1/2-inch slices
     2   medium yellow summer squash, cut into 1/2-inch
         slices
    12   cherry tomatoes
    12   pearl onions
     1   cup barbecue sauce
Hot cooked rice

On metal or soaked bamboo skewers, alternate meatballs, zucchini, summer squash, tomatoes and onions. Grill, uncovered, over medium heat for 6 minutes, turning once. Baste with barbecue sauce. Grill 8-10 minutes longer or until meatballs are heated through and vegetables are tender, turning and basting frequently. Serve over rice.

Yield: 5 servings.

Another Meaty Meal

Keep frozen fully cooked meatballs in the freezer as a quick meal starter for a recipe like this:

Thaw 2 pounds frozen meatballs; place in a 3-qt. microwave-safe dish. Top with 1 sliced small onion, 2 small julienned carrots, 1 small julienned green pepper and 1 minced garlic clove.

Combine 4-1/2 teaspoons soy sauce and a 10-ounce jar sweet-and-sour sauce; pour over meatballs.

Cover and microwave on high for 8-10 minutes or until vegetables are tender and meatballs are heated through, stirring twice.

Chili Cheese Turnovers

Prep: 15 min. **Bake:** 15 min.

2 tubes (10 ounces *each*) refrigerated pizza crust
2 cups (8 ounces) shredded Mexican cheese blend
1 can (15 ounces) chili without beans
1 can (15 ounces) ranch-style beans *or* chili beans, drained
1 can (10 ounces) diced tomatoes and green chilies, drained
1 cup (8 ounces) sour cream

On a lightly floured surface, press pizza dough into two 12-in. squares. Cut each into four 6-in. squares. In a bowl, combine the cheese, chili and beans. Spoon 1/2 cup in the center of each square. Fold dough diagonally over filling; press edges to seal.

Place in two greased 15-in. x 10-in. x 1-in. baking pans. Bake at 425° for 13-18 minutes or until golden brown. Cool for 5 minutes. Meanwhile, in a small bowl, combine tomatoes and sour cream. Serve with turnovers.

Yield: 8 servings.

Italian Turnovers

For a change of taste, give Chili Cheese Turnovers an Italian twist.

Toss some chopped pepperoni slices into your favorite spaghetti sauce. Sprinkle with shredded mozzarella cheese; stir.

Assemble and bake the turnovers as directed. Heat the remaining spaghetti sauce and serve on the side.

Spicy Shepherd's Pie

Prep/Total Time: 30 min.

1	package (6.6 ounces) instant mashed potatoes
1	pound ground beef
1	medium onion, chopped
1	can (14-1/2 ounces) diced tomatoes, undrained
1	can (11 ounces) Mexicorn, drained
1	can (2-1/4 ounces) sliced ripe olives, drained
1	envelope taco seasoning
1-1/2	teaspoons chili powder
1/2	teaspoon salt
1/8	teaspoon garlic powder
1	cup (4 ounces) shredded cheddar cheese, *divided*

Prepare mashed potatoes according to package directions. Meanwhile, in a large skillet, cook beef and onion over medium heat until meat is no longer pink; drain. Add tomatoes, corn, olives, taco seasoning, chili powder, salt and garlic powder. Bring to a boil; cook and stir for 1-2 minutes.

Transfer to a greased 2-1/2-qt. baking dish. Top with 3/4 cup cheese. Spread mashed potatoes over the top; sprinkle with remaining cheese. Bake, uncovered, at 350° for 12-15 minutes or until cheese is melted.

Yield: 4-6 servings.

Substitution Secret

If you prefer, replace the instant mashed potatoes with 4-1/2 cups hot mashed potatoes (prepared with milk and butter). Either make homemade mashed potatoes or buy some frozen or refrigerated potatoes.

Chili Beef Noodle Skillet

Prep/Total Time: 30 min.

   1 package (8 ounces) egg noodles
   2 pounds ground beef
   1 medium onion, chopped
 1/4 cup chopped celery
   2 garlic cloves, minced
   1 can (28 ounces) diced tomatoes, undrained
   1 tablespoon chili powder
 1/4 to 1/2 teaspoon salt
 1/8 teaspoon pepper
 1/2 to 1 cup shredded cheddar cheese

Cook noodles according to package directions. Meanwhile, in a large skillet, cook beef, onion, celery and garlic over medium heat until meat is no longer pink and vegetables are tender; drain. Add tomatoes, chili powder, salt and pepper; mix well. Cook and stir for 2 minutes.

Drain noodles; stir into beef mixture and heat through. Remove from the heat. Sprinkle with cheese; cover and let stand for 5 minutes or until cheese is melted.

Yield: 8 servings.

Preparation Pointer

You can cut fat and calories in this recipe by using yolk-free noodles, ground turkey breast and reduced-fat cheddar cheese.

Serving Suggestion

A vegetable side dish is all you need to round out this hearty skillet supper.

Either prepare your family's favorite canned or frozen variety.

Or simply offer a selection of fresh veggies and dip.

Beefy Biscuit Cups

Prep/Total Time: 30 min.

- 1 pound ground beef
- 1 jar (14 ounces) spaghetti sauce
- 2 tubes (8 ounces *each*) large refrigerated biscuits
- 1 cup (4 ounces) shredded cheddar cheese

In a skillet, cook beef over medium heat until no longer pink; drain. Stir in spaghetti sauce; cook over medium heat for 5-10 minutes or until heated through. Press biscuits onto the bottom and up the sides of greased muffin cups. Spoon 2 tablespoons meat mixture into the center of each cup.

Bake at 375° for 15-17 minutes or until golden brown. Sprinkle with cheese; bake 3 minutes longer or until the cheese is melted.

Yield: 8 servings.

Super Substitution

For a meatless entree or fast snack, fill these biscuit cups with canned baked beans. Sprinkle with shredded cheddar cheese. Bake as directed.

Bacon Cheeseburger Pasta

Prep/Total Time: 20 min.

8 ounces uncooked tube *or* spiral pasta
1 pound ground beef
6 bacon strips, diced
1 can (10-3/4 ounces) condensed tomato soup, undiluted
1 cup (4 ounces) shredded cheddar cheese
Barbecue sauce and prepared mustard, optional

Cook pasta according to package directions. Meanwhile, in a skillet, cook beef over medium heat until no longer pink; drain and set aside.

In the same skillet, cook bacon until crisp; remove with a slotted spoon to paper towels. Discard drippings. Drain pasta; add to the skillet. Add the soup, beef and bacon; heat through. Sprinkle with cheese; cover and cook until the cheese is melted. Serve with barbecue sauce and mustard if desired.

Yield: 4-6 servings.

Basil Cherry Tomatoes (p. 273)

Do-Ahead Idea

If you have time the night before, cook the ground beef and bacon as directed. Combine with the soup. Transfer to a covered container; refrigerate.

The next day, cook the pasta. Meanwhile, reheat the beef and bacon mixture in a skillet. Drain the pasta, add to the skillet and continue with the recipe as directed.

Nacho Pie

Prep/Total Time: 30 min.

- 4 cups nacho tortilla chips, coarsely crushed
- 1 pound ground beef
- 1/2 cup chopped onion
- Salt and pepper to taste
- 1 can (15-1/2 ounces) chili beans
- 1 can (8 ounces) tomato sauce
- 1 cup (4 ounces) shredded mozzarella cheese

Place chips in a lightly greased 9-in. pie plate and set aside. In a skillet over medium heat, cook beef and onion until meat is no longer pink; drain. Season with salt and pepper. Spoon over chips. Top with beans, tomato sauce and mozzarella. Bake, uncovered, at 375° for 15-17 minutes or until heated through.

Yield: 4-6 servings.

Crescent Crust

For a hearty crust, turn to an 8-ounce tube of refrigerated crescent rolls.

Separate crescent rolls into eight triangles; place in a greased 9-in. pie plate with points toward the center. Press onto the bottom and up the sides to form a crust; seal perforations.

Sprinkle 1 cup crushed chips over the crust. Top with all of the meat mixture, beans, tomato sauce and cheese. Bake at 350° for 20-25 minutes. Let stand 5 minutes before cutting.

Skillet Enchiladas

Prep/Total Time: 30 min.

- 1 pound ground beef
- 1 medium onion, chopped
- 1 can (10-3/4 ounces) condensed cream of mushroom soup, undiluted
- 1 can (10 ounces) enchilada sauce
- 1/3 cup milk
- 1 to 2 tablespoons canned chopped green chilies
  Vegetable oil
- 8 corn tortillas
- 2-1/2 cups (10 ounces) finely shredded cheddar cheese, *divided*
- 1/2 cup chopped ripe olives

In a large skillet, cook beef and onion over medium heat until meat is no longer pink; drain. Stir in the soup, enchilada sauce, milk and chilies. Bring to a boil. Reduce heat; cover and simmer for 20 minutes, stirring occasionally.

Meanwhile, in another skillet, heat 1/4 in. of oil. Dip each tortilla in hot oil for 3 seconds on each side or just until limp; drain on paper towels. Top each tortilla with 1/4 cup cheese and 1 tablespoon olives. Roll up and place over beef mixture, spooning some of mixture over the enchiladas. Cover and cook until heated through, about 5 minutes. Sprinkle with remaining cheese; cover and cook until cheese is melted.

Yield: 8 enchiladas.

Timely Tip

The filling for Skillet Enchiladas can be made the night before and stored in an airtight container in the refrigerator; reheat before continuing with the recipe.

Tortilla Lesson

The main difference between corn and flour tortillas is that flour tortillas are made with fat (usually lard or shortening) and corn tortillas are not.

Easy Chow Mein

Prep: 15 min.   **Cook:** 4 hours

- 1 pound ground beef
- 1 medium onion, chopped
- 1 bunch celery, sliced
- 2 cans (14 ounces *each*)
     Chinese vegetables, drained
- 2 envelopes brown gravy mix
- 2 tablespoons soy sauce

Hot cooked rice

In a skillet, cook beef and onion over medium heat until meat is no longer pink; drain. Transfer to a slow cooker. Stir in the celery, Chinese vegetables, gravy mixes and soy sauce.

Cover and cook on low for 4 hours or until celery is tender, stirring occasionally. Serve over rice.

Yield: 8 servings.

Easy Asian Menu

Host a casual Oriental-themed dinner with friends. Start with an appetizer of frozen egg rolls. Set out hot mustard and sweet-sour sauce for dipping.

In addition to Easy Chow Mein, prepare Shrimp Fried Rice (p. 229).

For dessert, pick up a box of fortune cookies from the store…or stop by a local Chinese restaurant for fortune and almond cookies.

Zesty Macaroni Soup

Prep/Total Time: 30 min.

1 pound ground beef
1 medium onion, chopped
5 cups water
1 can (15 ounces) pinto beans, rinsed and drained
1 can (14-1/2 ounces) diced tomatoes, undrained
1 can (7 ounces) whole kernel corn, drained
1 can (4 ounces) chopped green chilies, optional
1/2 teaspoon ground mustard
1/2 teaspoon salt
1/8 teaspoon pepper
1 package (7-1/2 ounces) chili macaroni dinner mix
Salsa con queso dip

In a saucepan, cook beef and onion until meat is no longer pink; drain. Stir in water, beans, tomatoes, corn and chilies if desired. Stir in mustard, salt, pepper and contents of macaroni sauce mix.

Bring to a boil. Reduce heat; cover and simmer for 10 minutes. Stir in contents of macaroni packet. Cover and simmer 10-14 minutes longer or until macaroni is tender, stirring once. Serve with salsa con queso dip.

Yield: 8-10 servings (about 2-1/2 quarts).

Preparation Pointer

Con queso is a Spanish term meaning "with cheese."

Salsa con queso dip can be found in the international food section or snack aisle of most grocery stores.

Or make your own by melting process cheese and stirring in some salsa.

Sloppy Joe Under a Bun

Prep/Total Time: 30 min.

1-1/2 pounds ground beef
1 can (15-1/2 ounces) sloppy
  joe sauce
2 cups (8 ounces) shredded
  cheddar cheese
2 cups biscuit/baking mix
2 eggs, beaten
1 cup milk
1 tablespoon sesame seeds

In a skillet, cook beef until no longer pink; drain. Stir in sloppy joe sauce; mix well. Transfer to a lightly greased 13-in. x 9-in. x 2-in. baking dish; sprinkle with cheese.

In a bowl, combine biscuit mix, eggs and milk just until blended. Pour over cheese; sprinkle with sesame seeds. Bake, uncovered, at 400° for 25 minutes or until golden brown.

Yield: 8 servings.

Low-Calorie Options

To cut the fat and calories in this recipe, use ground turkey and reduced-fat biscuit/baking mix.

Say 'Cheese'

For even cheesier flavor, stir some shredded cheddar cheese into the biscuit mix before pouring it over the sloppy joe casserole.

Green Chili Burritos

Prep/Total Time: 30 min.

- 1 can (16 ounces) refried beans
- 8 flour tortillas (6 inches)
- 1/2 pound ground beef, cooked and drained
- 1 cup (4 ounces) shredded sharp cheddar cheese, *divided*
- 1 can (4-1/2 ounces) chopped green chilies

Spread refried beans over tortillas. Top each with beef and 2 tablespoons of cheese. Fold ends and sides over filling and roll up; place seam side down in a greased 13-in. x 9-in. x 2-in. baking dish. Sprinkle with chilies and remaining cheese. Bake, uncovered, at 350° for 20 minutes or until heated through.

Yield: 4 servings.

Baked Chimichangas

It's easy to turn Green Chili Burritos into crispy chimichangas.

Fill and roll up tortillas. Place seam side down in a greased baking dish.

In a small bowl, whisk 1 egg white and 2 teaspoons water; brush over the top. Bake at 350° for 20 minutes or until heated through. Sprinkle with chilies and remaining cheese. Return to the oven until the cheese is melted.

Best Barbecue Sandwiches

Prep/Total Time: 25 min.

4-1/2 pounds ground beef
1-1/2 cups chopped onion
2-1/4 cups ketchup
   3 tablespoons prepared
      mustard
   3 tablespoons
      Worcestershire sauce
   2 tablespoons vinegar
   2 tablespoons sugar
   1 tablespoon salt
   1 tablespoon pepper
 18 hamburger buns, split

In a Dutch oven, cook beef and onion until meat is no longer pink and onion is tender; drain. Combine ketchup, mustard, Worcestershire sauce, vinegar, sugar, salt and pepper; stir into beef mixture. Heat though. Serve on buns.

Yield: 18 servings.

Cooking for a Crowd?

A hearty batch of Best Barbecue Sandwiches is just the thing for casual gatherings with friends during the week.

Store-bought coleslaw, potato salad and chips are simple side dish ideas.

An ice cream sundae bar with all the fixings is a speedy sweet treat that never goes out of style.

Onion Salisbury Steak

Prep/Total Time: 25 min.

   1   pound ground beef
 1/2 teaspoon salt
 1/8 to 1/4 teaspoon pepper
   2   medium onions, thinly sliced
   4   slices bread, toasted
 1/4 cup all-purpose flour
1-1/2 cups water
   1   tablespoon beef bouillon granules

In a bowl, combine beef, salt and pepper; shape into four oval patties. In a skillet, brown patties on one side. Turn and add onions. Cook until meat is no longer pink.

Place toast on serving plates. Top each with onions and a beef patty; keep warm. Stir flour into skillet until blended. Gradually add water; stir in bouillon. Bring to a boil; cook and stir for 2 minutes or until thickened and bubbly. Serve over meat and onions.

Yield: 4 servings.

Simple Substitution

Instead of making the Salisbury steak patties from scratch, use pre-shaped hamburgers from your grocer's meat section or frozen hamburger patties.

Timely Tip

Skip the step of making the sauce to serve over these patties by topping with store-bought beef gravy that's been heated according to package directions.

Idaho Tacos

Prep/Total Time: 20 min.

1 pound ground beef
1 envelope taco seasoning
4 hot baked potatoes
1/2 cup shredded cheddar
   cheese
1 cup chopped green
   onions
Salsa, optional

In a large skillet, cook beef over medium heat until no longer pink; drain. Add taco seasoning; prepare according to package directions.

With a sharp knife, cut an X in the top of each potato; fluff pulp with a fork. Top with taco meat, cheese and onions. Serve with salsa if desired.

Yield: 4 servings.

Basic Baked Potatoes

Start cooking the potatoes in the microwave while you cook the ground beef for Idaho Tacos.

   Scrub and pierce the potatoes with a fork. Place on a microwave-safe plate. Microwave, uncovered, on high for 12-14 minutes or until tender, turning once.

French Bread Pizza

Prep/Total Time: 25 min.

  1/2 pound ground beef
    1 can (16 ounces) pizza sauce
    1 jar (8 ounces) sliced mushrooms, drained
    1 loaf (1 pound) French bread
    2 cups (8 ounces) shredded mozzarella cheese

In a medium skillet, cook beef over medium heat until no longer pink; drain. Stir in pizza sauce and mushrooms; set aside. Cut bread in half lengthwise, then into eight pieces. Spread meat sauce on bread; place on a greased baking sheet. Sprinkle with cheese. Bake, uncovered, at 400° for 10 minutes or until cheese is melted and bubbly.

Yield: 6-8 servings.

Homemade Dressing

Few store-bought salad dressings can compare with one that's made from scratch. The following recipe for creamy peppercorn dressing can be stored covered in the refrigerator for up to 2 weeks.

In a small bowl, combine 1 cup mayonnaise, 1 cup (8 ounces) sour cream, 1/3 cup grated Parmesan cheese, 1/4 cup milk, 3 tablespoons lemon juice, 1-1/2 teaspoons coarsely ground pepper, 1/2 teaspoon salt and 1/2 teaspoon onion powder. Mix well.

Gaucho Casserole

Prep/Total Time: 30 min.

1   pound ground beef
1   medium onion, chopped
1   small green pepper,
     chopped
1   can (16 ounces) kidney
     beans, rinsed and drained
1   can (14-1/2 ounces) diced
     tomatoes, undrained
1   can (8 ounces) tomato sauce
1/4 cup water
1   envelope taco seasoning
1   teaspoon chili powder
1-1/3 cups uncooked instant rice
1   cup (4 ounces) shredded
     Mexican cheese blend

Crumble the beef into an ungreased 2-1/2-qt. microwave-safe dish. Add onion and green pepper; mix well. Cover and microwave on high for 6 minutes or until meat is no longer pink, stirring every 2 minutes; drain.

Stir in the beans, tomatoes, tomato sauce, water, taco seasoning and chili powder. Cover and microwave on high for 5-6 minutes or until bubbly, stirring every 2 minutes. Stir in rice.

Transfer to a shallow 2-1/2-qt. microwave-safe dish coated with nonstick cooking spray. Cover and let stand for 6-8 minutes or until liquid is absorbed. Sprinkle with cheese. Cover and microwave on high for 1-2 minutes or until cheese is melted.

Editor's Note: This recipe was tested in an 850-watt microwave.

Yield: 8 servings.

Choice Cheese

Mexican cheese blends give your recipes an authentic flavor by combining a blend of Mexican cheeses.

If you can't find Mexican cheese blend at the store, substitute shredded Monterey Jack, mild cheddar or Muenster cheeses or a combination of these cheeses.

Tomato Hamburger Topping

Prep/Total Time: 25 min.

1 pound ground beef

1 medium onion, chopped

1 medium green pepper, chopped

1 medium tomato, seeded and chopped

1 cup water

1 can (6 ounces) tomato paste

1/2 teaspoon garlic powder

1/2 teaspoon salt

1/4 teaspoon pepper

Hot cooked wild and long grain rice

In a large skillet, cook the beef and onion over medium heat until meat is no longer pink; drain. Add the green pepper, tomato, water, tomato paste, garlic powder, salt and pepper. Simmer, uncovered, for 15 minutes or until heated through. Serve over rice.

Yield: 3 cups.

Seeding a Tomato

To seed a tomato, first cut it in half. Carefully cut out the seeds and pulp with a paring knife. Chop the tomato as directed.

Serving Suggestions

Prepare a corn bread/muffin mix as directed; cool and cut into squares. Spoon Tomato Hamburger Topping over the top.

Or pour the topping over any variety of hot cooked pasta.

Pronto Pizza Burgers

Prep/Total Time: 25 min.

1/3 cup grated Parmesan cheese
1 tablespoon chopped onion
1 tablespoon tomato paste
1 teaspoon dried oregano
1/2 teaspoon salt
1/2 teaspoon pepper
1 pound ground beef
4 English muffins, split
8 tomato slices
8 mozzarella cheese slices
Additional oregano, optional

In a bowl, combine the first six ingredients; crumble beef over mixture and mix well. Toast the muffins in broiler until lightly browned. Form meat into four patties; place on top of muffins.

Broil 4 in. from the heat for 8-10 minutes or until meat is cooked. Top with tomato and cheese slices. Return to broiler until cheese is melted. If desired, sprinkle with oregano. Serve immediately.

Yield: 4 servings.

Great Greens

If you don't want to keep salad fixings on hand, stop by the grocery store to pick up fresh torn greens and cut-up vegetables from the salad bar.

Simple Substitution

Eight hamburger bun bottoms can be used in place of the split English muffins. Save the hamburger bun tops to make garlic bread to serve with another dinner.

Savory Winter Soup

Prep: 20 min.   **Cook:** 8 hours

2 pounds ground beef

3 medium onions, chopped

1 garlic clove, minced

3 cans (10-1/2 ounces *each*) condensed beef broth, undiluted

1 can (28 ounces) diced tomatoes, undrained

3 cups water

1 cup *each* diced carrots and celery

1 cup fresh *or* frozen cut green beans

1 cup cubed peeled potatoes

2 tablespoons minced fresh parsley *or* 2 teaspoons dried parsley flakes

1 teaspoon dried basil

1/2 teaspoon dried thyme

Salt and pepper to taste

In a skillet, cook beef, onions and garlic over medium heat until the meat is no longer pink; drain. Transfer to a 5-qt. slow cooker. Add the remaining ingredients and mix well. Cover and cook on high for 8 hours or until heated through.

Yield: 14 servings (3-1/2 quarts).

Preparation Pointer

Ever find parsley gets past its prime before you can use it all? Try this:

Thoroughly wash parsley and shake off excess moisture. Wrap in paper towels, then in a plastic bag; refrigerate. Parsley should stay fresh like this for about a week.

Mexican Chip Casserole

Prep/Total Time: 20 min.

1   pound ground beef
1   medium onion, chopped
1   garlic clove, minced
1   can (10-3/4 ounces)
     condensed cream of
     mushroom soup, undiluted
1   can (11 ounces) Mexicorn,
     drained
1   can (4 ounces) chopped
     green chilies, drained
1   package (10-1/2 ounces)
     corn chips
1   can (10 ounces) enchilada
     sauce
1   to 2 cups (4 to 8 ounces)
     shredded Colby-Monterey
     Jack cheese

In a skillet, cook beef, onion and garlic over medium heat until meat is no longer pink and onion is tender; drain. Add soup, corn and chilies; mix well. In an ungreased shallow 3-qt. baking dish, layer meat mixture, corn chips and enchilada sauce; top with cheese. Bake, uncovered, at 350° for 8-10 minutes or until heated through.

Yield: 6 servings.

Fruity Finale

Fresh fruit coated with a light lime dressing is a luscious, light way to end a Mexican meal.

In a large bowl, combine 3 cups cubed honeydew melon, 2 cups cubed watermelon, 2 cups cubed cantaloupe and 1/2 cup seedless red grapes.

Whisk together 2 tablespoons vegetable oil, 2 tablespoons lime juice, 1 tablespoon honey and 1/4 teaspoon grated lime peel. Pour over fruit and toss.

Favorite Meat Loaf Cups

Prep/Total Time: 30 min.

2 eggs, beaten
1/4 cup milk
1/4 cup ketchup
1/2 cup crushed cornflakes
4 tablespoons dried
  minced onion
1 teaspoon prepared
  mustard
1 teaspoon salt
1/4 teaspoon pepper
2 pounds ground beef
Additional ketchup, optional

In a large bowl, combine the first eight ingredients. Crumble beef over mixture and mix well. Press into 12 foil-lined or greased muffin cups. Bake at 350° for 25 minutes or until the meat is no longer pink. Drain before serving. Drizzle with ketchup if desired.

Yield: 6 servings.

Preparation Pointer

Use lean ground beef when making these meat loaf cups so you'll have less fat to pour off.

Quick Cornflake Crumbs

For 1/2 cup crushed cornflakes, start with 1-1/2 cups whole cornflakes. Or use purchased cornflake crumbs.

Salsa Chili

Prep/Total Time: 15 min.

1 pound ground beef
1 medium onion, chopped
1 jar (16 ounces) salsa
1 can (15 ounces) pinto beans, rinsed and drained
1 can (5-1/2 ounces) tomato juice
Shredded cheddar cheese, diced peppers, sour cream and
    sliced green onions, optional

In a saucepan, cook beef and onion over medium heat until
meat is no longer pink; drain. Stir in salsa, beans and tomato juice;
heat through. If desired, garnish with cheese and peppers and
serve with sour cream and onions.

Yield: 5 servings.

Serving Suggestions

For Cincinnati-style chili,
serve Salsa Chili over hot
cooked spaghetti.

Or for a fun way to pre-
sent hot dogs, spoon some
chili on top.

Substitution Secrets

Try substituting ground
beef with ground turkey.
Instead of pinto beans, use
black or kidney beans.
Replace regular tomato
juice with a spicy variety.

You don't have to wait for the weekend to cook beef. These recipes use quick-cooking cuts for hearty meals in minutes!

Flavorful Beef Stir-Fry
(p. 69)

Quick & Easy **Beef**

Beef Barley Stew (p. 54)

Festive Fillets (p. 56)

Sweet and Savory Brisket

Prep: 10 min.   **Cook:** 8 hours

1	beef brisket (3 to 3-1/2 pounds), cut in half
1	cup ketchup
1/4	cup grape jelly
1	envelope onion soup mix
1/2	teaspoon pepper

Place half of the brisket in a slow cooker. In a bowl, combine the ketchup, jelly, soup mix and pepper; spread half over meat. Top with the remaining meat and ketchup mixture. Cover and cook on low for 8-10 hours or until meat is tender. Slice brisket; serve with cooking juice.

Editor's Note: This is a fresh beef brisket, not corned beef.

Yield: 8-10 servings.

Tasty Taters

Speed up the preparation of mashed potatoes by using unpeeled red potatoes.

Cut 6 medium unpeeled red potatoes (about 1-1/2 pounds) into 1-in. pieces. Place in a saucepan; cover with water. Cover pan and bring to a boil. Reduce heat; cook for 10-15 minutes or until tender; drain well.

Add 1/3 to 1/2 cup warm heavy whipping cream, 2 tablespoons butter, 1/2 teaspoon salt and 1/4 teaspoon pepper. Coarsely mash the potatoes.

Steaks and Onions

Prep/Total Time: 30 min.

2 large onions, halved and
    sliced
1/4 cup butter
2/3 cup white wine *or*
    chicken broth
2 garlic cloves, minced
1 teaspoon dried rosemary,
    crushed
1/2 teaspoon salt
1/2 teaspoon pepper
4 beef tenderloin steaks
    (1-1/2 to 2 inches thick)

In a large skillet, cook onion in butter over medium heat for 15-20 minutes or until onions are golden brown, stirring frequently. Stir in wine or broth and garlic. Bring to a boil. Reduce heat; simmer, uncovered, for 3-4 minutes or until liquid has evaporated.

Meanwhile, combine the rosemary, salt and pepper; rub over steaks. Broil 4 in. from the heat for 7-9 minutes on each side or until meat reaches desired doneness (for medium-rare, a meat thermometer should read 145°; medium, 160°; well-done, 170°). Serve with caramelized onions.

Yield: 4 servings.

Quick Carrots

Colorful spiced carrot strips pair nicely with Steaks and Onions.

First julienne 5 large carrots and then place in a saucepan; cover with water. Cook for 8-10 minutes or until tender; drain.

Melt 2 tablespoons butter; combine with 1 tablespoon sugar, 1 teaspoon salt and 1/4 teaspoon ground cinnamon. Pour over carrots; toss to coat.

Corned Beef and Cabbage Sandwiches

Prep/Total Time: 10 min.

  1/3 cup mayonnaise
    1 tablespoon vinegar
  1/4 teaspoon ground mustard
  1/4 teaspoon celery seed
  1/4 teaspoon pepper
1-1/2 cups thinly shredded raw cabbage
    4 kaiser *or* hard rolls, split
  3/4 to 1 pound fully cooked corned beef, sliced

In a bowl, combine mayonnaise, vinegar, mustard, celery seed and pepper until smooth. Stir in cabbage and mix well. Spoon onto the bottom halves of rolls. Cover with corned beef; replace tops of rolls.

Yield: 4 servings.

Cabbage Capers

Instead of buying a head of cabbage and shredding it at home, pick up a package of coleslaw mix.

Set aside 1-1/2 cups for this recipe. Then store leftovers in the original bag and refrigerate in the crisper drawer.

Use remaining coleslaw mix in Chicken Noodle Stir-Fry (p. 95) or Southwestern Fish Tacos (p. 240).

You can also substitute shredded lettuce for the cabbage.

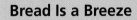

Skillet Steak and Corn

Prep/Total Time: 30 min.

1   **pound boneless round steak, cut into strips**
1   **medium onion, cut into 1/4-inch wedges**
1/2 **teaspoon dried thyme**
2   **tablespoons vegetable oil**
3/4 **cup red wine *or* beef broth**
1   **can (14-1/2 ounces) diced tomatoes, undrained**
2   **cans (11 ounces *each*) Mexicorn, drained**
Hot cooked rice

In a skillet or wok over medium-high heat, brown steak, onion and thyme in oil. Add wine or broth; simmer for 10 minutes or until the liquid has evaporated. Stir in tomatoes; cover and simmer 15 minutes longer. Add the corn and heat through. Serve over rice.

Yield: 4 servings.

Bread Is a Breeze

Refrigerated corn bread twists would make a nice accompaniment to Skillet Steak and Corn.

Or purchase a prepared corn bread from your grocer's bakery counter.

Beef Barley Stew

Prep: 20 min.   **Cook:** 6 hours

1-1/2 pounds beef stew meat,
       cut into 1-inch pieces
    1 medium onion, chopped
    2 tablespoons vegetable oil
    1 quart water
    1 can (15 ounces) tomato
       sauce
    5 medium carrots, cut into
       1/2-inch pieces
    1 celery rib, thinly sliced
    2 teaspoons salt
  1/2 teaspoon dried oregano
  1/2 teaspoon paprika
  1/4 teaspoon pepper
    2 cups fresh *or* frozen green beans
    2 cups fresh *or* frozen corn
  3/4 cup medium pearl barley

In a skillet, brown beef and onion in oil; drain. Transfer to a 5-qt. slow cooker. Add water, tomato sauce, carrot, celery, salt, oregano, paprika and pepper.

Cover and cook on low for 4-5 hours. Add beans, corn and barley; cover and cook on low 2 hours longer or until barley, beef and vegetables are tender.

Yield: 6-8 servings.

Meat for Beef Stew

The best beef for stew comes from less tender, well-marbled meat (like chuck and round), which will deliver a richer taste. Look for packages of cubed stew meat in the meat section of your grocery store.

Time-Saving Tip

Assemble the ingredients for Beef Barley Stew the night before. Slice the carrots and celery; refrigerate in a covered container. Also, measure the salt, oregano, paprika and pepper. Place in a small bowl; cover with plastic wrap.

No-Fuss Swiss Steak

Prep: 10 min.   **Cook:** 6 hours

 3 pounds boneless beef round steak, cut into serving-size pieces
 2 tablespoons vegetable oil
 2 medium carrots, cut into 1/2-inch slices
 2 celery ribs, cut into 1/2-inch slices
 1-3/4 cups water
 1 can (11 ounces) condensed tomato rice soup, undiluted
 1 can (10-1/2 ounces) condensed French onion soup, undiluted
 1/2 teaspoon pepper
 1 bay leaf

In a large skillet, brown beef in oil over medium-high heat; drain. Transfer to a 5-qt. slow cooker. Add carrots and celery. Combine the remaining ingredients; pour over meat and vegetables. Cover and cook on low for 6-8 hours or until meat is tender. Discard the bay leaf before serving. Thicken cooking juices if desired.

Yield: 8-10 servings.

Easy and Instant!

Offer your family a down-home dinner of No-Fuss Swiss Steak and mashed potatoes. The trick is to start with one package (7.5 ounces) roasted garlic instant mashed potatoes!

Bring 3 cups water and 1 cup milk to a rolling boil in a large saucepan. Remove from the heat and add the contents of both envelopes from the potato package. Let stand for 1 minute; whip with a fork.

Stir 4 ounces cubed, softened cream cheese into the potatoes. Transfer to a greased 1-qt. baking dish. Sprinkle with 1 cup cheddar cheese.

Festive Fillets

Prep/Total Time: 20 min.

> 1 envelope brown gravy mix
> 1 jar (4-1/2 ounces) sliced mushrooms, drained
> 2 teaspoons prepared horseradish
> 4 beef tenderloin steaks (5 ounces *each*)
> 1/8 teaspoon pepper

Prepare gravy according to package directions; add mushrooms and horseradish. Set aside and keep warm. In a nonstick skillet, cook fillets over medium-high heat until meat reaches desired doneness (about 10-13 minutes for medium), turning once. Season with pepper. Serve with gravy.

Yield: 4 servings.

Oven-Baked Steaks

For added convenience, Festive Fillets can also be baked. First brown the steaks in a skillet for 1 minute on each side.

Transfer to an 8-in. square baking pan. Bake, uncovered, at 350 for 10-20 minutes or until meat reaches desired doneness.

Herbed Potato Wedges (p. 278)

Pineapple Beef Stir-Fry

Prep/Total Time: 30 min.

- 1/2 **cup soy sauce**
- 2 **garlic cloves, minced**
- 1 **teaspoon ground ginger**
- 1 **pound boneless beef sirloin steak, cut into 1/4-inch thin strips**
- 1 **tablespoon vegetable oil**
- 2 **celery ribs, thinly sliced**
- 1 **cup cubed sweet red pepper**
- 1 **cup sliced green onions**
- 1 **cup sliced fresh mushrooms**
- 1 **can (20 ounces) pineapple chunks**
- 1 **can (8 ounces) sliced water chestnuts, drained**
- 2 **to 3 tablespoons cornstarch**
- 1/2 **cup water**

Hot cooked rice

In a bowl, combine the soy sauce, garlic and ginger. Add beef; toss to coat. Let stand for 15 minutes. In a large skillet, stir-fry beef mixture in oil for 2 minutes. Add celery and red pepper; stir-fry for 2 minutes. Add onions and mushrooms; cook 2 minutes longer.

Drain pineapple, reserving juice. Stir pineapple and water chestnuts into skillet. In a bowl, combine cornstarch, water and reserved pineapple juice until smooth. Gradually stir into beef and vegetables. Bring to a boil; cook and stir for 1-2 minutes or until thickened. Serve over rice.

Yield: 4 servings.

Rely on Rice

Rice is a staple side dish to serve with stir-fry. When making rice, plan on 1/2 cup per person.

Keep in mind that 1 cup instant rice will yield 2 cups cooked. One cup converted rice equals about 3-1/2 cups cooked. And 1 cup brown rice yields 4 cups cooked.

Grilled Roast Beef Sandwiches

Prep/Total Time: 30 min.

1 medium onion, sliced

1 medium green pepper, sliced

1/2 pound fresh mushrooms, sliced

2 to 3 garlic cloves, minced

2 tablespoons vegetable oil

1/4 teaspoon salt

1/8 teaspoon pepper

8 slices sourdough bread

16 slices Colby-Monterey Jack *or* Swiss cheese, *divided*

8 slices deli roast beef

1/2 cup butter, softened

Garlic salt, optional

In a large skillet, saute the onion, green pepper, mushrooms and garlic in oil until tender; sprinkle with salt and pepper. On four slices of bread, layer two slices of cheese, two slices of beef and a fourth of the vegetable mixture. Top with the remaining cheese and bread.

Butter outside of bread; sprinkle with garlic salt if desired. On a hot griddle, toast sandwiches for 3-4 minutes on each side or until golden brown.

Yield: 4 servings.

Special Sides

When you go to the store to pick up the fixings for the Grilled Roast Beef Sandwiches, also pick up potato chips or prepared potato salad to serve on the side.

For dessert, purchase brownies or cookies from your store's bakery.

Reuben Chowder

Prep/Total Time: 30 min.

1 tablespoon butter, softened
3 slices rye bread
1 can (11 ounces) condensed nacho cheese soup, undiluted
1 can (10-3/4 ounces) condensed cream of mushroom soup, undiluted
3 cups milk
1 can (14 ounces) sauerkraut, rinsed and drained
12 ounces deli corned beef, diced
1 cup (4 ounces) shredded mozzarella cheese

Butter bread on both sides; cube. Place on an ungreased baking sheet. Bake at 375° for 6-8 minutes or until browned.

Meanwhile, in a large saucepan, combine the soups, milk, sauerkraut and corned beef; cook and stir over medium heat for 8-10 minutes or until heated through. Add cheese; stir until melted. Top with croutons.

Yield: 8 servings (2 quarts).

Crouton Tip

You can make the rye bread croutons for this chowder days in advance. When cool, store in an airtight container at room temperature.

Although you only need three slices of bread for the croutons, rye bread (unlike other types of bread) has a long shelf life and can be kept for several weeks. Use the leftovers in a variety of sandwiches or serve buttered slices with the soup.

Beef Chow Mein

Prep/Total Time: 15 min.

4 teaspoons cornstarch
1 teaspoon sugar
4 teaspoons soy sauce
1 garlic clove, minced
1/2 pound beef tenderloin, cut into thin strips
1 tablespoon vegetable oil
2 cups uncooked vegetables (carrots, green pepper, broccoli, celery, cauliflower *and/or* green onions)
1/3 cup beef broth
Chow mein noodles *or* hot cooked rice

In a bowl, combine the first four ingredients. Add beef and toss to coat. In a large skillet or wok, stir-fry beef in oil until no longer pink; remove and keep warm.

Reduce heat to medium. Add vegetables and broth; stir-fry for 4 minutes. Return beef to the pan; cook and stir for 2 minutes or until heated through. Serve over chow mein noodles or rice.

Yield: 2 servings.

Preparation Pointer

Check your grocer's produce aisle for packages of fresh vegetables that have already been cleaned and cut up.

Serving Suggestion

Skip the standard white rice you normally serve with stir-fry and set out chow mein noodles.

Chow mein noodles are egg noodles that have been fried, giving them a delicious crunchy texture.

One 5-ounce can yields 2-1/2 cups.

Green Pepper Steak

Prep/Total Time: 30 min.

1/4 cup soy sauce
1/4 cup water
1 tablespoon cornstarch
2 to 3 tablespoons vegetable oil, *divided*
1 pound boneless beef sirloin steak, thinly sliced
2 small onions, thinly sliced and separated into rings
1 green pepper, cut into 1-inch pieces
2 celery ribs, sliced diagonally
2 tomatoes, cut into wedges
Hot cooked rice

For sauce, combine soy sauce, water and cornstarch; set aside. Heat 1 tablespoon of oil in a large skillet or wok over high heat. Stir-fry half of the beef until browned. Remove and repeat with remaining beef, adding additional oil as needed. Remove meat and keep warm. Add onions, green pepper and celery to pan; stir-fry until crisp-tender, about 3-4 minutes. Return beef to pan.

Stir the sauce; add to pan. Cook and stir until thickened and bubbly. Cook and stir 2 minutes more. Add tomatoes; cook just until heated through. Serve over rice.

Yield: 4 servings.

Celery Secrets

Look for crisp, green celery stalks with fresh leaves.

Refrigerate in a plastic bag for up to 10 days, leaving the ribs attached to the stalks. Wash just before using.

To remove the strings from tough celery stalks, snap a 1/2-in. length at the top so it's still hanging on. Then pull the piece down the length of the rib.

Grilled Peppered Steaks

Prep/Total Time: 25 min.

> 1-1/2 to 2 teaspoons coarsely ground pepper
> 1 teaspoon onion salt
> 1 teaspoon garlic salt
> 1/4 teaspoon paprika
> 4 New York strip steak (about 8 ounces *each*)

In a small bowl, combine the pepper, onion salt, garlic salt and paprika if desired. Rub onto both sides of steaks. Grill, covered, over medium heat for 8-10 minutes on each side or until meat reaches desired doneness (for medium-rare, a meat thermometer should read 145°; medium, 160° well-done, 170°).

Yield: 4 servings.

Simple Sauteed Mushrooms

Most folks agree a steak dinner just isn't complete without some sauteed mushrooms.

In a large skillet, melt 1/4 cup butter. Add 1 pound sliced fresh mushrooms, 1 tablespoon lemon juice and 1 tablespoon soy sauce.

Saute for 6-8 minutes or until mushrooms are tender.

Great Garden Veggies (p. 262)

Easy Beef Goulash

Prep/Total Time: 30 min.

1-1/2 cups uncooked spiral pasta
1 pound boneless sirloin steak, cut into 1/8-inch-thick strips
1 tablespoon vegetable oil
1 medium onion, chopped
1 medium green pepper, chopped
1 can (14-1/2 ounces) diced tomatoes, undrained
1-1/2 cups water
1 cup beef broth
1-1/2 teaspoons red wine vinegar
1 to 2 teaspoons paprika
1 teaspoon sugar
1/2 teaspoon salt
1/4 teaspoon caraway seeds
1/4 teaspoon pepper
2 tablespoons all-purpose flour
1/4 cup cold water

Cook pasta according to package directions. Meanwhile, in a large nonstick skillet, stir-fry beef in oil for 4-5 minutes or until browned. Add onion and green pepper; cook and stir for 2 minutes. Stir in tomatoes, water, broth, vinegar and seasonings. Bring to boil. Reduce heat; cover and simmer for 15 minutes.

In a small bowl, combine flour and cold water until smooth. Add to skillet. Bring to a boil; cook and stir for 2 minutes or until thickened. Drain pasta; stir into beef mixture.

Yield: 6 servings.

Simple Side Salad

While the goulash is simmering, combine 3 tablespoons cider vinegar, 1/2 cup shredded Parmesan cheese and 1/2 teaspoon garlic powder in a blender or food processor.

Cover and process until combined. Gradually add 1/3 cup olive oil in a steady stream. Place 7 cups torn romaine in a salad bowl; drizzle with dressing. Toss to coat and serve immediately.

Ginger Beef Stir-Fry

Prep/Total Time: 25 min.

    3   tablespoons cornstarch, *divided*
    2   tablespoons water
  1/4   teaspoon salt
1-1/2   pounds boneless beef sirloin steak, thinly sliced
        into 3-inch strips
    2   tablespoons vegetable oil, *divided*
  3/4   cup thinly sliced carrots
  3/4   cup beef broth
    2   tablespoons soy sauce
    2   teaspoons grated orange peel
    1   teaspoon ground ginger
Hot cooked rice

In a large bowl, combine 2 tablespoons cornstarch, water and salt until smooth. Add beef; toss to coat. In a large skillet, stir-fry beef in batches in 1 tablespoon oil until meat reaches desired doneness; remove and keep warm.

Stir-fry carrots in remaining oil for 5-6 minutes. Place remaining cornstarch in a bowl; stir in broth until smooth. Add the soy sauce, orange peel and ginger.

Return beef to skillet; stir in broth mixture. Bring to a boil. Cook and stir for 2 minutes or until thickened. Serve over rice.

Yield: 4 servings.

Go with Gingerroot

Consider using fresh gingerroot to flavor dishes.

Buy fresh gingerroot in the produce section. If tightly wrapped, gingerroot stays fresh in the freezer for up to 6 months.

To use, remove the brown skin with a vegetable peeler. Rub the peeled part of the root against the fine holes of a metal grater.

One tablespoon of fresh gingerroot is roughly equivalent to 1 teaspoon of ground ginger.

Philly Steak Sandwiches

Prep/Total Time: 30 min.

- 1/2 pound fresh mushrooms, sliced
- 2 medium onions, thinly sliced
- 1 medium green pepper, sliced
- 2 tablespoons butter
- 1 pound thinly sliced cooked roast beef
- 6 hoagie rolls, split
- 6 slices (8 ounces) mozzarella cheese
- 4 beef bouillon cubes
- 2 cups water

In a skillet, saute mushrooms, onions and green pepper in butter until tender. Divide beef among rolls. Top with vegetables and cheese; replace roll tops. Place on an ungreased baking sheet; cover with foil. Bake at 350° for 15 minutes or until heated through.

In a small saucepan, heat bouillon and water until cubes are dissolved; serve as a dipping sauce.

Yield: 6 servings.

Jiffy Au Jus

Instead of making your own au jus dipping sauce with bouillon cubes, pick up a can of au jus and prepare as directed.

Cheese Steak Story

It's said the authentic cheese steak sandwich was invented by an Italian immigrant in South Philadelphia in the 1930s.

Many versions exist across the country, but they all feature thinly sliced beef on a hoagie roll.

Artichoke Beef Steaks

Prep/Total Time: 25 min.

1 jar (6-1/2 ounces) marinated
   artichoke hearts
4 boneless beef rib eye steaks
   (3/4 inch thick and about
   8 ounces *each*)
1/2 teaspoon salt
2 tablespoons butter
1 small onion, sliced and
   separated into rings
1 garlic clove, minced
1 jar (2 ounces) sliced pimientos,
   drained

Drain artichokes, reserving 1 tablespoon marinade. Cut artichokes in half and set aside.

Sprinkle steaks with salt. In a large skillet, cook steaks in butter over medium-high heat for 4 minutes on each side or until the meat reaches desired doneness (for medium-rare, a meat thermometer should read 145°; medium, 160°; well-done, 170°). Remove to a serving platter; keep warm.

In same skillet, saute the onion and garlic in reserved marinade for 3 minutes. Add the artichokes and pimientos; heat through. Serve over steaks.

Yield: 4 servings.

Hurry-Up Herbed Bread

While the steaks are cooking in the skillet, prepare herbed French bread.

Cut a 1-pound loaf of French bread into 1-in. slices. In a small bowl, combine 1/2 cup softened butter, 1/4 cup minced fresh parsley and 1/4 cup minced chives; spread over one side of each slice of bread.

Place bread buttered side up on an ungreased baking sheet. Broil 4 in. from the heat for 1-2 minutes or until golden brown.

Flank Steak Stir-Fry

Prep/Total Time: 20 min.

    4 **teaspoons cornstarch**
2/3 **cup beef broth**
    2 **tablespoons soy sauce**
1/4 **teaspoon pepper**
    1 **pound beef flank steak, cut into 1/4-inch strips**
1-1/2 **cups fresh *or* frozen broccoli florets**
    1 **cup sliced fresh mushrooms**
1/2 **cup julienned sweet red pepper**
1/2 **cup julienned carrot**
1/4 **teaspoon ground ginger**
    2 **tablespoons vegetable oil**
Hot cooked rice

In a small bowl, combine the cornstarch, broth, soy sauce and pepper until smooth; set aside. In a skillet, stir-fry the beef, broccoli, mushrooms, red pepper, carrot and ginger in oil until meat is no longer pink and vegetables are crisp-tender. Stir broth mixture; add to the skillet. Bring to a boil; cook and stir for 2 minutes or until thickened. Serve over rice.

Yield: 4 servings.

Preparation Pointer

Any combination of frozen mixed vegetables can be substituted for the broccoli, mushrooms, red pepper and carrot.

Broccoli, carrots and water chestnuts; broccoli, cauliflower and pepper or cauliflower, carrots and snow peas are just a few of the combinations you'll find in your grocer's frozen food aisle.

Dijon Mushroom Beef

Prep/Total Time: 20 min.

1/2 pound fresh mushrooms, sliced
  1 medium onion, sliced
  2 teaspoons olive oil
  1 pound boneless beef sirloin steak, thinly sliced
  1 can (10-3/4 ounces) condensed cream of
     mushroom soup, undiluted
3/4 cup milk
  2 tablespoons Dijon mustard
Hot cooked egg noodles, optional

In a large nonstick skillet, saute mushrooms and onion in oil until tender. Remove and set aside. In the same skillet, cook beef until no longer pink. Add the soup, milk, mustard and mushroom mixture. Bring to a boil. Reduce heat; cook and stir until thickened. Serve over hot cooked noodles if desired.

Yield: 4 servings.

Stock-Up Secret

Stock your freezer for fast future meals by purchasing sirloin steak when you see it on sale.

Wrap it tightly in plastic wrap, place in a resealable plastic bag and freeze for up to 6 months.

When ready to use, remove the steak from the freezer and place on a plate in the refrigerator to thaw. For a 1-in. steak, allow about 12 hours.

Easy Slicing

It's easier to slice beef cuts like sirloin and round steak if you do so while the beef is partially frozen.

Flavorful Beef Stir-Fry

Prep/Total Time: 30 min.

2 tablespoons cornstarch
2 teaspoons sugar
6 tablespoons soy sauce
1/4 cup white wine, apple juice *or* water
1 pound boneless round steak, cut into thin strips
3 cups broccoli florets
2 medium carrots, thinly sliced
1 package (6 ounces) frozen pea pods, thawed
2 tablespoons chopped onion
2 tablespoons vegetable oil, *divided*
1 can (8 ounces) sliced water chestnuts, undrained
Hot cooked rice

In a bowl, combine cornstarch, sugar, soy sauce and wine, apple juice or water until smooth. Add beef and toss to coat; set aside.

In a large skillet, stir-fry broccoli, carrots, pea pods and onion in 1 tablespoon oil for 1 minute. Stir in water chestnuts. Cover and simmer for 4 minutes; remove and keep warm.

In the same skillet, stir-fry beef in remaining oil until meat reaches desired doneness. Return vegetables to pan; toss. Serve over rice.

Yield: 4 servings.

Broccoli Basics

A 1-pound head of broccoli yields approximately 3-1/2 cups florets.

No time to cut it up? Look for packages of fresh broccoli florets near the salad kits in your store's produce section.

Broiled Beef Kabobs

Prep/Total Time: 25 min.

- 1 tablespoon olive oil
- 1 tablespoon lemon juice
- 1 tablespoon water
- 2 teaspoon Dijon mustard
- 1 teaspoon honey
- 1/2 teaspoon dried oregano
- 1/4 teaspoon pepper
- 1 pound boneless top sirloin steak (1 inch thick), cut into 1-inch cubes
- 2 small green *and/or* sweet red peppers, cut into 1-inch pieces
- 12 large fresh mushrooms
- Hot cooked rice

In a bowl, combine the first seven ingredients; mix well. Add beef, peppers and mushrooms; toss to coat. Thread meat and vegetables alternately on metal or soaked wooden skewers.

Broil 3 in. from the heat, turning often, until meat reaches desired doneness and vegetables are tender, about 12-16 minutes. Serve over rice.

Yield: 4 servings.

Grilled Potatoes

When weather allows, grill these kabobs outside along with the following potato side dish.

Dice 2 medium potatoes. Place in a purchased foil bag. Add 1 cup chopped onion, 2 tablespoons butter, 1/2 teaspoon salt and 1/4 teaspoon white pepper. Seal bag tightly. Grill for 20-30 minutes or until potatoes are tender.

Steak Diane

Prep/Total Time: 15 min.

4 beef rib eye steaks (1/2 inch thick)
1/4 teaspoon pepper
1/8 teaspoon salt
4 tablespoons butter, *divided*
2 tablespoons finely chopped green onions
1/2 teaspoon ground mustard
1 tablespoon lemon juice
1-1/2 teaspoons Worcestershire sauce
1 tablespoon minced fresh parsley
1 tablespoon minced fresh chives

Sprinkle steaks with pepper and salt. In a skillet, melt 2 tablespoons butter. Stir in onions and mustard; cook for 1 minute. Add steaks; cook for 2 minutes on each side or until the meat reaches desired doneness. Remove to a serving platter and keep warm. Add lemon juice, Worcestershire sauce and remaining butter to skillet; cook for 2 minutes. Add parsley and chives. Pour over steaks.

Yield: 4 servings.

Rice Makes It Nice

Here's an easy recipe for herbed rice.

In a saucepan over medium heat, melt 2 tablespoons butter for about 2 minutes or until golden brown, stirring often.

Stir in 3 cups uncooked instant rice, 3 cups water, 3 teaspoons chicken bouillon granules and 1/2 teaspoon poultry seasoning.

Bring to a boil. Remove from the heat; cover and let stand for 5 minutes. Fluff with a fork.

Slow Cooker Barbecue Beef

Prep: 15 min.   **Cook:** 8 hours

- 1 boneless beef sirloin tip roast (about 3 pounds), cut into large chunks
- 3 celery ribs, chopped
- 1 large onion, chopped
- 1 medium green pepper, chopped
- 1 cup ketchup
- 1 can (6 ounces) tomato paste
- 1/2 cup packed brown sugar
- 1/4 cup cider vinegar
- 3 tablespoon chili powder
- 2 tablespoons lemon juice
- 2 tablespoons molasses
- 2 teaspoons salt
- 2 teaspoons Worcestershire sauce
- 1 teaspoon ground mustard
- 8 to 10 sandwich rolls, split

Place beef in a 5-qt. slow cooker. Add the celery, onion and green pepper. In a bowl, combine the ketchup, tomato paste, brown sugar, vinegar, chili powder, lemon juice, molasses, salt, Worcestershire sauce and mustard. Pour over beef mixture. Cover and cook on low for 8-9 hours or until meat is tender.

Skim fat from cooking juices if necessary. Shred beef. Toast rolls if desired. Use a slotted spoon to serve beef on rolls.

Yield: 8-10 servings.

Lively Leftovers

This recipe for barbecue beef makes a big batch that gives you a head start for a meal in the future.

Just freeze half of the cooked meat in a freezer-safe container. Pull it out of the freezer on a busier-than-normal night.

Or for lively lunches for one, freeze some of the meat in single-serving portions.

Steak Stir-Fry

Prep/Total Time: 25 min.

1 teaspoon beef bouillon granules
1 cup boiling water
2 tablespoons cornstarch
1/3 cup soy sauce
1 pound boneless sirloin steak, cut into thin strips
1 garlic clove, minced
1 teaspoon ground ginger
1/4 teaspoon pepper
2 tablespoons vegetable oil, *divided*
1 large green pepper, julienned
1 cup sliced carrots *or* celery
5 green onions, cut into 1-inch pieces

Hot cooked rice

Dissolve bouillon in water. Combine the cornstarch and soy sauce until smooth; add to bouillon. Set aside. Toss beef with garlic, ginger and pepper. In a large skillet or wok over medium-high heat, stir-fry beef in 1 tablespoon oil until cooked as desired; remove and keep warm. Heat remaining oil; stir-fry vegetables until crisp-tender.

Stir soy sauce mixture and add to the skillet; bring to a boil. Cook and stir for 2 minutes. Return meat to pan and heat through. Serve over rice.

Yield: 4 servings.

Green Onion Know-How

Green onions can vary in thickness and length. When using large pieces in recipes, look for more slender varieties. Those no larger than 1/2 inch in diameter are best.

Look for green onions with a crisp, bright green top and a firm white base.

Refrigerate unwashed green onions in a plastic bag for about 5 days.

Cube Steak Skillet Supper

Prep/Total Time: 30 min.

1/2	cup all-purpose flour
1/2	teaspoon salt

Dash pepper

4	cube steaks
2	to 4 tablespoons vegetable oil
2	small onions, sliced
2	cans (15 ounces *each*) sliced potatoes, drained
2	cans (14-1/2 ounces *each*) French-style green beans, drained
2	cans (10-3/4 ounces *each*) condensed golden mushroom soup, undiluted

Paprika

In a large resealable plastic bag, combine flour, salt and pepper. Add steaks and shake to coat. In a skillet, brown steaks on both sides in oil. Set aside and keep warm. Add onion, potatoes and beans to skillet; stir in soup. Return steaks to skillet. Cover and simmer for 15 minutes or until meat is tender. Sprinkle with paprika.

Yield: 4 servings.

Dependable Dessert

For a quick dessert, dress up a frozen New York-style cheesecake.

Combine 1/2 cup milk chocolate toffee bits and 1/4 cup caramel ice cream topping. Spread over the cheesecake.

For a simple chocolate creation, dust slices with cocoa powder.

Or open a can of your favorite pie filling (like cherry, apple or blueberry) and spoon it on top of individual slices.

Roast Beef Roll-Ups

Prep/Total Time: 15 min.

- 1/2 **cup sour cream**
- 1/4 **cup mayonnaise**
- 1/4 **cup salsa**
- 10 **flour tortillas (8 inches)**
- 1 **pound thinly sliced cooked roast beef**
- 10 **large lettuce leaves**

Additional salsa

Combine sour cream, mayonnaise and salsa; spread over tortillas. Top with roast beef and lettuce. Roll up tightly and secure with toothpicks; cut in half. Serve with salsa.

Yield: 10 servings.

Taste Twists

For a more intense Southwestern flavor in Roast Beef Roll-Ups, use a flavored mayonnaise, such as a hot and spicy variety.

Or try any kind of flavored flour tortillas, like spinach, whole wheat or tomato-basil.

Peppery Beef Stir-Fry

Prep/Total Time: 25 min.

      8 ounces uncooked linguine
      1 tablespoon cornstarch
      1 teaspoon pepper
    1/4 teaspoon cayenne pepper
      1 cup water
    1/2 cup soy sauce
  1-1/2 pounds boneless beef sirloin steak, cut into
         thin strips
      2 tablespoons vegetable oil
    1/2 cup julienned green pepper
    1/2 cup julienned sweet red pepper
      2 to 3 garlic cloves, minced
      2 cups fresh *or* frozen snow peas, thawed and halved
      2 cups sliced fresh mushrooms

Cook linguine according to package directions; drain. In a small bowl, combine the cornstarch, pepper and cayenne. Stir in water and soy sauce until smooth; set aside.

In a large nonstick skillet or wok, stir-fry beef in hot oil for 4-5 minutes or until no longer pink. Using a slotted spoon, remove meat and set aside. Add the peppers and garlic; stir-fry for 1 minute. Add the snow peas and mushrooms; stir-fry for 2-3 minutes or until vegetables are crisp-tender.

Stir soy sauce mixture and add to vegetables. Bring to a boil; cook and stir for 2 minutes or until thickened. Stir in beef and linguine; heat through.

Yield: 6 servings.

Know Your Peas & Qs!

Snow peas (also known as Chinese pea pods) are flat and thin; sugar snap peas are plump with prominent peas.

Avoid buying pods that are limp or broken and that are not bright green or are not crisp.

Store unwashed snow and sugar snap peas in a plastic bag in the refrigerator for up to 3 days.

Before using, wash and snap off the stem ends.

Steaks with Squash Medley

Prep/Total Time: 30 min.

2 rib eye steaks (10 ounces *each*)
3 tablespoons olive oil, *divided*
1/2 cup chopped onion
1/2 cup chopped yellow summer squash
1/2 cup chopped zucchini
1/2 cup sliced okra, optional
1 garlic clove, minced
1/4 cup tomato sauce
3 tablespoons white vinegar
1/2 teaspoon dried rosemary, crushed
1/2 teaspoon dried thyme
1/8 teaspoon pepper

In a skillet over medium heat, brown steaks on both sides in 2 tablespoons oil. Cook 8 minutes longer or until the meat reaches desired doneness (for medium-rare, a meat thermometer should read 145°; medium, 160°; well-done, 170°). Remove and keep warm.

Drain skillet. Saute onion, squash, zucchini, okra if desired and garlic in remaining oil for 6 minutes or until tender. Stir in the tomato sauce, vinegar, rosemary, thyme and pepper. Cook 3-4 minutes longer or until heated through. Serve over steaks.

Yield: 2 servings.

Preparation Pointer

Yellow summer squash and zucchini are available year round and add freshness and color to a variety of dishes.

Keep unwashed squash in a sealed plastic bag in the crisper drawer for up to 4 days.

Steak Fajitas

Prep/Total Time: 30 min.

- 2 medium tomatoes, seeded and diced
- 1/2 cup diced red onion
- 1/4 cup lime juice
- 3 tablespoons minced fresh cilantro
- 1 jalapeno pepper, seeded and chopped
- 2 teaspoons ground cumin
- 1/2 teaspoon salt
- 1 beef flank steak (about 1-1/2 pounds)
- 1 large onion, halved and sliced
- 1 tablespoon vegetable oil
- 6 flour tortillas (6 inches), warmed

Canned black beans and guacamole

In a bowl, combine the first seven ingredients. Cover and refrigerate. Broil or grill steak over medium-hot heat for 6-8 minutes on each side or until meat reaches desired doneness (for medium-rare, a meat thermometer should read 145°; medium, 160°; well-done, 170°).

Meanwhile, in a skillet, saute onion in oil until crisp-tender. Slice steak into thin strips across the grain; place on tortillas. Top with onion and the reserved tomato relish. Serve with black beans and guacamole.

Editor's Note: When cutting or seeding hot peppers, use rubber or plastic gloves to protect your hands. Avoid touching your face.

Yield: 6 servings.

Refried Favorites

Zesty refried beans are a change of pace from ordinary black beans and a perfect complement to Steak Fajitas.

In a saucepan, combine 2 cans (16 ounces each) refried beans, 1 jar (8 ounces) salsa and 1/2 teaspoon ground cumin; cook until heated through. Serve with sour cream if desired.

Slow-Cooked Rump Roast

Prep: 10 min.   **Cook:** 10-1/2 hours

1	boneless beef rump roast (3 to 3-1/2 pounds)
2	tablespoons vegetable oil
4	medium carrots, halved lengthwise and cut into 2-inch pieces
3	medium potatoes, peeled and cut into chunks
2	small onions, sliced
1/2	cup water
6	to 8 tablespoons horseradish sauce
1/4	cup red wine vinegar
1/4	cup Worcestershire sauce
2	garlic cloves, minced
1-1/2	to 2 teaspoons celery salt
3	tablespoons cornstarch
1/3	cup cold water

Cut roast in half. In a large skillet, brown meat on all sides in oil over medium-high heat; drain. Place carrots and potatoes in a 5-qt. slow cooker. Top with meat and onions. Combine the water, horseradish sauce, vinegar, Worcestershire sauce, garlic and celery salt. Pour over meat. Cover and cook on low for 10-12 hours or until meat and vegetables are tender.

Combine cornstarch and cold water until smooth; stir into slow cooker. Cover and cook on high for 30 minutes or until gravy is thickened.

Yield: 6-8 servings.

Browning Is Better

While it's not necessary to brown meat before placing it in the slow cooker, doing so imparts more flavor.

A Toast to Roasts

Rump roast comes from the round and is an economical cut that's perfect for family dining.

Many round and chuck cuts can be used interchangeably in recipes.

Take advantage of this fact when the cut specified in a recipe is not available or when certain cuts are on sale.

Busy cooks can depend on chicken when they want to offer their families a flavorful variety of entrees throughout the year.

Sesame Ginger Chicken
(p. 119)

Cookin' with Chicken

Baked Chicken
Quesadillas (p. 102)

Country Barbecued Chicken

Prep/Total Time: 15 min.

3/4 cup ketchup
1 tablespoon molasses
2 teaspoons brown sugar
1 teaspoon chili powder
1 teaspoon vegetable oil
1/2 teaspoon Worcestershire sauce
1 garlic clove, minced
1-1/2 to 2 pounds boneless skinless
chicken breast halves
2 tablespoons butter, melted

In a small bowl, combine the first seven ingredients. Cover and refrigerate until ready to use. Brush chicken with butter. Grill, uncovered, over medium-hot heat for 3-4 minutes on each side or until browned. Baste with barbecue sauce. Continue basting and turning for 4-6 minutes or until meat juices run clear.

Yield: 4-6 servings (3/4 cup barbecue sauce).

Preparation Pointer

Brush on thick or sweet sauces during the last 10-15 minutes of grilling, basting and turning every few minutes to prevent overbrowning.

Serving Suggestion

If you'd like, make a double batch of the barbecue sauce and reserve half of it to serve at the table.

The thick, zesty sauce is also equally tasty over grilled pork chops.

Lemon Chicken and Rice

Prep/Total Time: 30 min.

1   pound boneless skinless chicken
    breasts, cut into strips
1   medium onion, chopped
1   large carrot, thinly sliced
2   garlic cloves, minced
2   tablespoons butter
1   tablespoon cornstarch
1   can (14-1/2 ounces) chicken broth
2   tablespoons lemon juice
1/2 teaspoon salt
1-1/2 cups uncooked instant rice
1   cup frozen peas

In a skillet, cook chicken, onion, carrot and garlic in butter for 5-7 minutes or until chicken is no longer pink.

In a bowl, combine cornstarch, broth, lemon juice and salt until smooth. Add to skillet; bring to a boil. Cook and stir for 2 minutes or until thickened. Stir in rice and peas. Remove from the heat; cover and let stand for 5 minutes.

Yield: 6 servings.

Fresh Is Better

Fresh lemon juice will enhance the flavor of this chicken dish more than bottled juice. One medium lemon yields about 2 tablespoons juice.

You'll be able to get more juice out of a lemon that's at room temperature. If you're working with a cold lemon, microwave it for a few seconds or roll it on the countertop with your hand a few times.

Chicken Salsa Pizza

Prep/Total Time: 15 min.

1 prebaked Italian bread shell crust (14 ounces)
2 cups (8 ounces) shredded cheddar cheese, *divided*
1 jar (11 ounces) salsa
1 cup cubed cooked chicken

Place bread shell on an ungreased 12-in. pizza pan. Sprinkle with 3/4 cup of cheese. Top with salsa, chicken and remaining cheese. Bake at 450° for 8-10 minutes or until cheese is bubbly.

Yield: 4 servings.

Bread Shell Basics

Italian bread shell crusts come in original, thin and whole wheat varieties.

Select a shell that will please your family's palate.

Substitution Ideas

A blend of shredded Mexican cheeses can be used in place of the cheddar cheese.

Or consider making Italian Chicken Pizza by using mozzarella cheese for the cheddar and spaghetti sauce for the salsa.

Broiled Ginger Chicken

Prep/Total Time: 20 min.

    4 boneless skinless chicken breast halves
       (about 1 pound)
  1/2 cup mayonnaise
    1 tablespoon soy sauce
  1/4 teaspoon ground ginger
  1/8 teaspoon cayenne pepper

Flatten the chicken to 1/4-in. thickness. Place on a broiler pan rack. Broil for 3 minutes on each side. Combine mayonnaise, soy sauce, ginger and cayenne; brush over chicken. Broil 2-3 minutes longer on each side or until juices run clear.

Yield: 4 servings.

Flattening Chicken Breasts

Boneless skinless chicken breasts will cook more evenly if they're first flattened to a uniform thickness.

To easily flatten them, place in a resealable plastic bag; close the bag.

Lay the bag flat on the counter. Pound the chicken with the flat side of a meat mallet, working from the center of each chicken breast.

If you do this when you bring chicken home from the store and then freeze them, the chicken will thaw faster and be ready to use!

Stir-Fried Cabbage (p. 269)

Honey-Mustard Chicken Kabobs

Prep/Total Time: 30 min.

4 boneless skinless chicken
   breast halves
4 small zucchini
4 small yellow squash
2 medium sweet red peppers
4 ounces small fresh
   mushrooms

GLAZE:
   3/4 cup honey
   1/2 cup prepared mustard
   1/4 cup water
   2 tablespoons soy sauce
   2 tablespoons cornstarch
   1 tablespoon cider vinegar
Hot cooked rice, optional

Cut chicken, squash and peppers into 1-in. pieces; thread along with mushrooms alternately onto metal or soaked wooden skewers. In a saucepan, combine glaze ingredients; bring to a boil. Boil for 1 minute or until thickened.

Grill the kabobs over hot heat for 10 minutes, turning often. Brush with the glaze; grill 5 minutes more or until the chicken is no longer pink and the vegetables are tender. Serve over rice if desired.

Yield: 4 servings.

Fast Finale

Buy a pan of prepared brownies at the bakery. Cut into squares; top with your favorite ice cream. Drizzle with chocolate syrup or caramel ice cream topping.

Make-Ahead Idea

You can cut up the chicken, squash and peppers the night before. Assemble the kabobs as directed; place on a large backing pan and cover with foil; refrigerate. The glaze can also be prepared in advance; let cool, cover and chill.

Smothered Chicken

Prep/Total Time: 20 min.

4 boneless skinless chicken breast halves
    (4 ounces *each*)
Garlic powder and seasoned salt to taste
1 tablespoon vegetable oil
1 jar (4-1/2 ounces) sliced mushrooms, drained
1 cup (4 ounces) shredded Mexican cheese blend
1/2 cup chopped green onions
1/2 cup bacon bits

Flatten chicken to 1/4-in. thickness. Sprinkle with garlic powder and seasoned salt. In a large nonstick skillet over medium heat, brown chicken in oil for 4 minutes; turn. Top with the mushrooms, cheese, green onions and bacon. Cover and cook until chicken juices run clear and cheese is melted, about 4 minutes.

Yield: 4 servings.

Speedy Side Dish

Place 7 cups fresh or frozen broccoli florets and 1/4 cup water in a microwave-safe bowl. Cover; cook on high for 5-7 minutes or until crisp-tender.

Meanwhile, combine 2 tablespoons olive oil, 1 tablespoon lemon juice, 2 minced garlic cloves, 1 teaspoon salt and 1 teaspoon hot pepper sauce.

Drain broccoli and drizzle with lemon juice mixture; toss to coat.

Artichoke Chicken Pizza

Prep/Total Time: 25 min.

1 sheet frozen puff pastry, thawed
1 pound boneless skinless chicken breast, cubed
1 medium onion, halved and thinly sliced
2 tablespoons olive oil
2 cans (14-1/2 ounces *each*) diced tomatoes, well drained
2 jars (6-1/2 ounces *each*) marinated artichoke hearts, drained and coarsely chopped
1 can (2-1/4 ounces) sliced ripe olives, drained
3/4 teaspoon dried oregano
3/4 cup prepared Alfredo sauce
3/4 cup shredded Monterey Jack cheese

On a lightly floured surface, roll out pastry into a 15-in. x 10-in. x 1-in. rectangle. Transfer to an ungreased 15-in. x 10-in. x 1-in. baking pan. Prick pastry thoroughly with a fork. Bake at 400° for 11-13 minutes or until lightly browned.

Meanwhile, in a large skillet, saute chicken and onion in oil until chicken juices run clear. Stir in the tomatoes, artichokes, olives and oregano. Remove from the heat.

Spread Alfredo sauce over crust. With a slotted spoon, spoon chicken mixture over sauce; sprinkle with the cheese. Bake for 5 minutes or until cheese is melted.

Yield: 6-8 servings.

Saucy Apricot Chicken

Prep: 5 min.   **Cook:** 4 hours

6   boneless skinless chicken breast halves
    (about 1-1/2 pounds)
2   jars (12 ounces *each*) apricot preserves
1   envelope onion soup mix
Hot cooked rice

Place chicken in a slow cooker. Combine the preserves and soup mix; spoon over chicken. Cover and cook on low for 4-5 hours or until tender. Serve over rice.

Yield: 6 servings.

Slow Cooker Secrets

While dinner is cooking in the slow cooker, avoid the temptation to lift the lid and sneak a peek!

The loss of steam can mean an additional 15 to 30 minutes of cooking each time you remove the cover. Also be sure the lid is seated properly and is not ajar.

For food safety reasons, remove food from the slow cooker within 1 hour after it's finished cooking.

Parmesan Chicken

Prep/Total Time: 15 min.

  4 boneless skinless chicken breast halves
     (4 ounces *each*)
1/2 cup seasoned bread crumbs
1/4 cup grated Parmesan cheese
1/2 teaspoon dried basil
  1 egg
  1 tablespoon butter
  1 tablespoon vegetable oil

Flatten chicken to 1/4-in. thickness. In a shallow bowl, combine bread crumbs, Parmesan cheese and basil. In another bowl, beat the egg. Dip chicken into egg, then coat with crumb mixture. In a large skillet, brown chicken in butter and oil over medium heat for 3-5 minutes on each side or until juices run clear.

Yield: 4 servings.

Preparation Pointer

Blot the chicken dry with paper towel before dipping it into the egg. This will help the coating adhere to the chicken while cooking.

Side Dish Idea

Keep a box of frozen breadsticks on hand. Take out as many breadsticks as needed and bake while you're preparing the Parmesan Chicken.

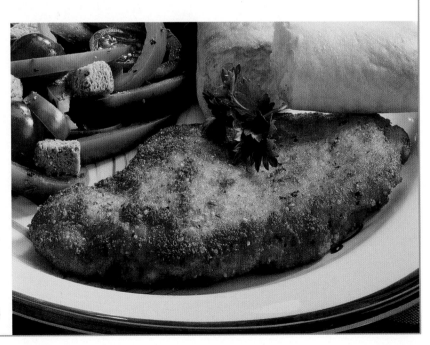

Italian Vegetable Saute (p. 258)

Cheesy Chicken Subs

Prep/Total Time: 25 min.

- 12 ounces boneless skinless chicken breasts, cut into strips
- 1 envelope Parmesan Italian *or* Caesar salad dressing mix
- 1 cup sliced fresh mushrooms
- 1/2 cup sliced red onion
- 1/4 cup olive oil
- 4 submarine buns, split and toasted
- 4 slices Swiss cheese

Place chicken in a bowl; sprinkle with salad dressing mix. In a skillet, saute mushrooms and onion in oil for 3 minutes. Add chicken; saute for 6 minutes or until chicken juices run clear.

Spoon mixture onto roll bottoms; top with cheese. Broil 4 in. from the heat for 4 minutes or until cheese is melted. Replace tops.

Yield: 4 servings.

Cooking Chicken Strips

When cutting the chicken for Cheesy Chicken Subs, be sure to make strips of uniform size.

For easier slicing, cut the chicken before it is completely thawed. And use a kitchen scissors instead of a knife.

After handling raw chicken, wash the scissors, cutting board, countertop and your hands thoroughly with hot, soapy water.

Quick Comforting Chicken

Prep/Total Time: 30 min.

- 1 pound boneless skinless chicken breasts, cut into strips
- 1 medium onion, sliced and separated into rings
- 1-1/2 cups frozen baby carrots, thawed
- 1/2 cup butter
- 1 can (15 ounces) small whole potatoes, drained
- 1 cup heavy whipping cream
- 1 tablespoon dried parsley flakes
- 1/2 teaspoon salt
- 1/4 teaspoon pepper

In a large skillet or Dutch oven, cook chicken, onion and carrots in butter until chicken is lightly browned. Add potatoes. Cover and cook over medium heat for 10 minutes or until the carrots are tender. Add the cream, parsley, salt and pepper. Reduce heat. Simmer, uncovered, for 10 minutes or until slightly thickened.

Yield: 4 servings.

Timely Tip

When you want to serve old-fashioned fare during the week, reach for this down-home classic!

With convenient canned potatoes, frozen baby carrots and quick-cooking chicken breasts, there's little prep work.

While this one-pot meal is simmering, toss together a simple green salad and set out some bakery dinner rolls.

Honey Barbecue Chicken

Prep/Total Time: 30 min.

1   can (20 ounces) pineapple chunks
4   boneless skinless chicken breast halves (4 ounces each)
1   teaspoon curry powder
1   tablespoon vegetable oil
1/2   cup chopped onion
1/2   cup chopped green pepper
1   bottle (18 ounces) honey barbecue sauce
Hot cooked rice

Drain pineapple, reserving juice; set fruit and juice aside. Sprinkle chicken with curry powder. In a large skillet, brown chicken on both sides in oil over medium-high heat. Remove and keep warm.

In the same skillet, saute the onion, green pepper and pineapple until vegetables are tender and pineapple is golden brown. Stir in barbecue sauce and reserved pineapple juice. Return chicken to the pan. Cover and simmer for 15 minutes or until chicken juices run clear. Serve over rice.

Yield: 4 servings.

Preparation Pointer

Not sure if your family will enjoy the flavor of curry? When you make this recipe for the first time, use only 1/2 teaspoon curry and see how they like it.

Simple Substitution

For even more color, replace half of the green pepper with sweet red pepper.

Italian Pineapple Chicken

Prep/Total Time: 20 min.

- 4 boneless skinless chicken breast halves
  (4 ounces *each*)
- 1/2 cup Italian salad dressing
- 2 tablespoons olive oil
- 1 can (8 ounces) sliced pineapple, drained
- 1/3 cup shredded Swiss cheese, optional

Flatten chicken to 1/2-in. thickness. Pour salad dressing into a shallow bowl; dip chicken in dressing. In a large skillet, heat oil. Add chicken; cook over medium-high heat for 5-7 minutes on each side or until juices run clear. Remove and keep warm.

Add pineapple slices to the skillet; cook for 30 seconds on each side or until lightly browned. Place a slice on each chicken breast half. Sprinkle with cheese if desired.

Yield: 4 servings.

Easy Meal Ending

A fruity, fluffy dessert pairs well with this skillet chicken dish.

Drain one can (14-1/2 ounces) tart cherries. In a bowl, combine the cherries and 1 tablespoon cherry gelatin powder. Fold in a thawed carton (8 ounces) frozen whipped topping. Chill until serving time.

Feta-Topped Asparagus (p. 266)

Chicken Noodle Stir-Fry

Prep/Total Time: 25 min.

1 package (3 ounces) chicken-flavored
  Ramen noodles
1 pound boneless skinless chicken
  breasts, cut into strips
1 tablespoon vegetable oil
1 cup broccoli florets
1 cup cauliflowerets
1 cup sliced celery
1 cup coarsely chopped cabbage
2 medium carrots, thinly sliced
1 medium onion, thinly sliced
1/2 cup fresh *or* canned bean sprouts
1/2 cup teriyaki *or* soy sauce

Set aside seasoning packet from noodles. Cook noodles according to package directions. Meanwhile, in a large skillet or wok, stir-fry chicken in oil for 5-6 minutes or until no longer pink.

Add vegetables; stir-fry for 3-4 minutes or until crisp-tender. Drain noodles; add to the pan with contents of seasoning packet and the teriyaki sauce. Stir well. Serve immediately.

Yield: 4 servings.

Preparation Pointer

All ingredients for a stir-fry should be cut up and ready to go before you begin cooking. If possible, do some prep work the night before.

Stir-Fry Secrets

When stir-frying meat, wait a few seconds before tossing so that it has a chance to brown. When cooking vegetables, begin stirring them as soon as you put them in the pan.

Herbed Chicken and Veggies

Prep: 20 min. **Cook:** 7-3/4 hours

- 1 broiler/fryer chicken (3 to 4 pounds), cut up and skin removed
- 2 medium tomatoes, chopped
- 1 medium onion, chopped
- 2 garlic cloves, minced
- 1/2 cup chicken broth
- 2 tablespoons white wine *or* additional chicken broth
- 1 bay leaf
- 1-1/2 teaspoons salt
- 1 teaspoon dried thyme
- 1/4 teaspoon pepper
- 2 cups broccoli florets

Hot cooked rice

Place chicken in a slow cooker. Top with tomatoes, onion and garlic. Combine broth, wine or additional broth, bay leaf, salt, thyme and pepper; pour over chicken. Cover and cook on low for 7-8 hours.

Add broccoli; cook 45-60 minutes longer or until the chicken juices run clear and the broccoli is tender. Discard bay leaf. Thicken pan juices if desired. Serve over rice.

Yield: 4-6 servings.

Bouillon for Broth

If you don't want to open a whole can of broth just for the 1/2 cup needed in this recipe, simply dissolve 1/2 teaspoon instant chicken bouillon granules in 1/2 cup hot water.

Skinny Tortilla Soup

Prep/Total Time: 30 min.

1 can (16 ounces) fat-free refried beans
1 can (15 ounces) black beans, rinsed and drained
1 can (14-1/2 ounces) reduced-sodium chicken broth
1-1/2 cups frozen corn
3/4 cup chunky salsa
3/4 cup cubed cooked chicken breast
1/2 cup water
2 cups (8 ounces) reduced-fat shredded cheddar
cheese, *divided*
28 baked tortilla chips, *divided*

In a large saucepan, combine the first seven ingredients. Bring to a boil. Reduce heat; cover and simmer for 10 minutes. Add 1 cup cheese; cook and stir over low heat until melted. Crumble half of the tortilla chips into soup bowls.

Ladle soup over chips. Top each serving with two crumbled chips; sprinkle with remaining cheese.

Yield: 7 servings.

Preparation Pointer

The next time you roast a whole chicken for Sunday dinner, put an extra bird in the oven.

Cube the leftover chicken and freeze in various portion sizes (1/2 cup, 3/4 cup and 1 cup).

Then during the week, you can remove a package from the freezer, defrost it and easily make any recipe calling for cubed cooked chicken.

Caesar Chicken Wraps

Prep/Total Time: 30 min.

1/2 cup Caesar salad dressing
1/2 cup grated Parmesan
      cheese, *divided*
  1 teaspoon lemon juice
  1 garlic clove, minced
1/4 teaspoon pepper
  1 package (8 ounces) cream
      cheese, softened
  3 cups shredded romaine
1/2 cup diced sweet red pepper
  1 can (2-1/4 ounces) sliced
      ripe olives, drained
  5 flour tortillas (10 inches)
1-3/4 cups cubed cooked chicken

In a small bowl, combine the salad dressing, 1/4 cup Parmesan cheese, lemon juice, garlic and pepper. In a small mixing bowl, beat cream cheese until smooth. Add half of the salad dressing mixture and mix well; set aside.

In a large bowl, combine the romaine, red pepper and olives. Add the remaining salad dressing mixture; toss to coat. Spread about 1/4 cup cream cheese mixture on each tortilla. Top with the romaine mixture and chicken; sprinkle with remaining Parmesan cheese. Roll up; cut in half.

Yield: 5 servings.

A Way with Wraps

Tortillas and pita breads are the breads most often used for sandwich wraps.

For easier rolling, first warm up the bread in the microwave to make them more pliable.

When time allows, roll up the wrap in plastic wrap and refrigerate a few hours. This enhances the flavor and helps the wrap stay rolled up when eating.

Rosemary Lime Chicken

Prep/Total Time: 20 min.

   4   boneless skinless chicken breast halves (5 ounces *each*)
   2   tablespoons vegetable oil
1/2   cup white wine *or* chicken broth
1/4   cup lime juice
   2   tablespoons minced fresh rosemary *or* 2 teaspoons dried rosemary, crushed
1/2   teaspoon salt
1/4   teaspoon pepper

Flatten chicken to 1/2-in. thickness. In a large skillet, brown chicken in oil over medium-high heat. Add the remaining ingredients. Cook, uncovered, for 5-7 minutes or until chicken juices run clear.

Yield: 4 servings.

Rosemary Facts

Supermarkets have fresh rosemary readily available year-round. The flavor is superior to dried rosemary, so use it when you can.

Look for fresh rosemary sprigs with leaves that are fragrant and green and that are not brittle or dry.

Refrigerate fresh rosemary in a plastic bag or in a glass of cold water. If rosemary wilts, revive it in an ice water bath.

Chili Chicken Strips

Prep/Total Time: 25 min.

3/4 cup crushed corn chips
2 tablespoons dry bread crumbs
1 tablespoon all-purpose flour
1 to 1-1/2 teaspoons chili powder
1/2 teaspoon seasoned salt
1/2 teaspoon poultry seasoning
1/4 teaspoon pepper
1/4 teaspoon paprika
1 egg
1-1/2 pounds boneless skinless chicken breasts, cut into 1/2-inch strips
4 tablespoons butter, *divided*

In a shallow bowl, combine the first eight ingredients. In another shallow bowl, beat egg. Dip chicken strips in egg, then coat with corn chip mixture.

In a large skillet, cook half of the chicken in 2 tablespoons butter for 8-10 minutes or until the juices run clear. Repeat with remaining chicken and butter.

Yield: 6 servings.

Chip Choices

To vary the flavor of Chili Chicken Strips, use different kinds of corn chips. Look for barbecue, honey barbecue, chili cheese and hot and spicy.

Serving Suggestion

You can serve these chicken strips with a variety of dipping sauces, like honey, barbecue sauce and ketchup.

Chicken Stir-Fry Bake

Prep/Total Time: 30 min.

2 cups uncooked instant rice
1 can (8 ounces) sliced water chestnuts, drained
2 cups cubed cooked chicken
1 package (16 ounces) frozen stir-fry vegetables, thawed
1 can (14-1/2 ounces) chicken broth
1/4 cup soy sauce
1 garlic clove, minced
1/2 to 3/4 teaspoon ground ginger

Preparation Pointer

One pound of boneless chicken yields about 3 cups cubed. Purchase a whole, 1-pound piece of cooked chicken breast from the deli and cube it.

Use 2 cups in this recipe. Set aside the remaining cup to make Chicken Salsa Pizza on page 84.

Place rice in an 11-in. x 7-in. x 2-in. baking dish. Layer with water chestnuts, chicken and vegetables. Combine remaining ingredients; pour over top. Cover and bake at 375° for 25 minutes or until rice is tender.

Yield: 4 servings.

Baked Chicken Quesadillas

Prep/Total Time: 15 min.

> 4 flour tortillas (8 inches)
> 1 package (6 ounces) ready-to-use Southwestern chicken strips
> 1 can (10 ounces) diced tomatoes and green chilies, well drained
> 1 cup (4 ounces) shredded Mexican cheese blend
> Shredded lettuce, sliced ripe olives and chopped tomatoes, optional

Coat one side of two tortillas with nonstick cooking spray; place coated side down on an ungreased baking sheet. Top each with chicken, tomatoes and cheese. Cover with remaining tortillas; spritz tops with nonstick cooking spray.

Bake at 450° for 10 minutes or until golden brown. Cut into wedges. Garnish with lettuce, olives and tomatoes if desired.

Yield: 2-4 servings.

Preparation Pointer

You can easily double the recipe for Baked Chicken Quesadillas for a larger group. Or serve them as appetizers at a party.

Speedy Strips

Ready-to-use chicken strips are located near the other packaged meats at your grocery store. They come in a variety of flavors and are handy for quick entrees and salads.

Tomato Artichoke Chicken

Prep/Total Time: 30 min.

1 jar (12 ounces) marinated artichoke hearts
4 boneless skinless chicken breast halves
1 tablespoon olive oil
2 cups pizza sauce
1 jar (7-1/4 ounces) roasted sweet red peppers, drained and cut into strips
Hot cooked fettuccine

Drain artichoke hearts, reserving 1/4 cup liquid. Cut artichokes into quarters. In a large skillet, brown chicken in oil. Add pizza sauce, artichokes, red peppers and reserved artichoke liquid. Bring to a boil. Reduce heat; cover and simmer for 8-10 minutes or until chicken juices run clear. Serve over fettuccine.

Yield: 4 servings.

Homemade Pizza Sauce

Instead of buying pizza sauce, make your own in just 45 minutes!

In a large saucepan, saute 3 minced garlic cloves in 3 tablespoons olive oil until tender.

Stir in one 29-ounce can tomato puree, one 28-ounce can crushed tomatoes, 2 tablespoons brown sugar, 1 tablespoon Italian seasoning, 1 teaspoon dried basil, 1/2 teaspoon salt and 1/2 teaspoon crushed red pepper flakes. Bring to a boil.

Reduce heat; simmer, uncovered, for 30 minutes or until thickened. Cover and refrigerate for up to 1 week.

Mushroom Chicken Fettuccine

Prep/Total Time: 15 min.

1 package (16 ounces) fettuccine
1 pound fresh mushrooms, sliced
4 garlic cloves, minced
1/4 cup butter
2 cans (5 ounces *each*) chunk white chicken, drained
1/2 cup milk
1-1/3 cups grated Parmesan cheese

Cook fettuccine according to package directions. Meanwhile, in a skillet, saute mushrooms and garlic in butter for 2-3 minutes. Add chicken and milk; cook for 5-7 minutes or until heated through. Drain fettuccine; add to the skillet. Sprinkle with the cheese and toss to coat.

Yield: 6 servings.

Reach for the Wheat

Pasta made from nutritionally superior whole-wheat flour is now available in a variety of shapes and sizes with a texture that is virtually identical to white flour pasta. (That means your kids won't know the difference!) So give it a try in this recipe.

Clubhouse Chicken

Prep/Total Time: 30 min.

8 boneless skinless chicken
   breast halves (2 pounds)
2 tablespoons vegetable oil
1 can (28 ounces) stewed
   tomatoes, cut up
1-1/2 cups sliced fresh mushrooms
1 large green pepper, julienned
1 medium onion, chopped
1/2 cup water
3 teaspoons Italian seasoning
1/4 teaspoon pepper
3 tablespoons all-purpose flour
1/4 cup cold water
Hot cooked rice

In a large skillet, brown chicken on both sides in oil. Stir in the tomatoes, mushrooms, green pepper, onion, water, Italian seasoning and pepper. Bring to a boil. Reduce heat; cover and simmer for 10-15 minutes or until chicken juices run clear.

Remove chicken and keep warm. Combine the flour and cold water until smooth; stir into tomato mixture. Bring to a boil; cook and stir for 2 minutes or until thickened. Serve chicken and sauce over rice.

Yield: 8 servings.

Tip for Thickeners

It's important that you combine flour (or cornstarch) with cold water before adding it to the hot liquid in the pan.

Whisk the thickening mixture into the pan and cook only for as long as directed. Overcooking can cause the thickener to thin again.

Sweet 'n' Tangy Chicken Sandwiches

Prep/Total Time: 20 min.

1/4 cup Dijon mustard
2 tablespoons honey
1 teaspoon dried oregano
1 teaspoon water
1/4 teaspoon garlic powder
1/8 to 1/4 teaspoon cayenne
   pepper
4 boneless skinless chicken
   breast halves (1 pound)
4 sandwich buns, split
8 thin tomato slices
1 cup shredded lettuce

In a bowl, combine the first six ingredients. Broil chicken 4 in. from the heat for 3 minutes on each side. Brush with mustard sauce. Broil 4-6 minutes longer or until juices run clear, basting and turning several times. Serve on buns with tomato and lettuce.

Yield: 4 servings.

Best Bean Salad

A cool bean salad is the perfect complement to these hot chicken sandwiches. Pick up a container from your grocer's deli counter.

Preparation Pointer

The chicken can also be grilled, covered, over medium heat for 6 to 10 minutes or each side or until juices run clear.

Strawberry Chicken Salad

Prep/Total Time: 30 min.

DRESSING:
- 1/2 cup honey
- 1/2 cup red wine vinegar
- 4 teaspoons soy sauce
- 1 garlic clove, minced
- 1/2 teaspoon ground ginger
- 1/4 teaspoon salt

Dash pepper

SALAD:
- 1 pound boneless skinless chicken breasts, cut into strips
- 1 tablespoon vegetable oil
- 1 teaspoon butter
- 8 cups torn mixed salad greens
- 1 pint fresh strawberries, sliced
- 1/4 cup chopped walnuts

Additional whole strawberries, optional

In a small bowl, combine the dressing ingredients. In a large skillet, cook and stir chicken in oil and butter until no longer pink; drain. Add 1/2 cup salad dressing; cook 1 minute longer.

Place the salad greens in a serving bowl. Top with chicken, sliced strawberries and walnuts. Garnish with whole strawberries if desired. Serve with remaining dressing.

Yield: 4 servings.

Strawberry Facts

Buy strawberries that are brightly colored and plump with the hulls still attached. Avoid soft, shriveled or moldy berries.

Wash berries before hulling. Refrigerate in a covered container.

One pint will yield about 2 cups sliced or chopped.

Chili with Chicken

Prep/Total Time: 30 min.

2 cans (15 ounces *each*) great northern beans,
   rinsed and drained
2 jars (16 ounces *each*) picante sauce
4 cups cubed cooked chicken
1 to 2 teaspoons ground cumin
Shredded Monterey Jack cheese

In a saucepan, combine beans, picante sauce, chicken and cumin. Bring to a boil. Reduce heat; cover and simmer for 20 minutes. Sprinkle individual servings with cheese.

Yield: 6 servings.

Tasty Toppings

The toppings for chili vary depending on the region of the country.

The most popular ideas include shredded cheese, sour cream, cooked macaroni, oyster crackers and chopped onion.

Don't forget to set a bottle of hot sauce on the table for folks who like things a little hotter.

Chicken Cacciatore

Prep/Total Time: 15 min.

1-1/2 pounds boneless skinless
      chicken breasts,
      cut into 1/2-inch strips
    1 medium onion, sliced and
      separated into rings
    1 medium green pepper,
      julienned
    2 tablespoons vegetable oil
    1 can (15 ounces) tomato
      sauce
    1 can (14-1/2 ounces)
      stewed tomatoes
    2 teaspoons garlic powder
  1/2 teaspoon dried oregano
  1/2 teaspoon salt
  1/2 teaspoon pepper
Hot cooked rice

In a skillet, cook the chicken, onion and green pepper in oil until chicken is lightly browned and vegetables are tender. Add tomato sauce, stewed tomatoes and seasonings; bring to a boil. Reduce heat; simmer, uncovered, for 5 minutes or until heated through. Serve over rice.

Yield: 6 servings.

Preparation Pointer

The taste of Chicken Cacciatore will be even more terrific if you make it the day before.

Serving Suggestion

For more authentic flavor, serve Chicken Cacciatore over any kind of hot cooked pasta.

Chicken with Pears and Squash

Prep: 10 min. **Cook:** 30 min.

1/4 cup plus 1 tablespoon
   all-purpose flour, *divided*
1/4 teaspoon salt
1/8 teaspoon white pepper
  4 boneless skinless chicken
   breast halves (4 ounces *each*)
  2 tablespoons plus 1 teaspoon
   vegetable oil, *divided*
  1 small onion, sliced
  2 cups cubed peeled butternut
   squash
  1 can (15-1/4 ounces) sliced pears
  1 cup chicken broth
1/4 teaspoon minced fresh thyme

In a large resealable plastic bag, combine 1/4 cup flour, salt and pepper. Add chicken, one piece at a time, and shake to coat. In a large skillet, brown chicken in 2 tablespoons oil on all sides; set aside.

In the same skillet, cook onion in remaining oil for 5 minutes or until tender. Drain pears, reserving syrup; set pears aside. In a small bowl, place the remaining flour; add the broth, thyme and reserved pear syrup until blended. Add to the skillet. Bring to a boil. Cook and stir for 2 minutes or until thickened.

Add the chicken and squash. Bring to a boil. Reduce heat to medium; cover and cook for 15-20 minutes or until chicken is no longer pink and squash is tender. Add reserved pears; cook until heated through.

Editor's Note: This recipe was tested in a 1,100-watt microwave.

Yield: 4 servings.

Butternut Basics

Butternut squash is a winter squash that's rich in complex carbohydrates and beta-carotene. It's also a good source of fiber, potassium and vitamin C.

When a recipe calls for cubed butternut squash, first use a chef's knife to cut it in half crosswise, at the point where the round bottom begins to narrow.

Cut each half into large chunks. Remove the peel with a smaller knife, then cut into cubes.

Soft Chicken Tacos

Prep/Total Time: 15 min.

1 pound boneless skinless chicken breasts, cut into cubes
1 can (15 ounces) black beans, rinsed and drained
1 cup salsa
1 tablespoon taco seasoning
6 flour tortillas (8 inches), warmed

OPTIONAL TOPPINGS:
Shredded lettuce, shredded cheddar cheese, sliced radishes, diced tomatoes, sliced green onions and sour cream

In a skillet coated with nonstick cooking spray, cook chicken until juices run clear. Add beans, salsa and taco seasoning; heat through. Spoon the chicken mixture down the center of each tortilla. Garnish with toppings of your choice.

Yield: 6 servings.

Serving Suggestion

Hominy is a nice side dish to serve with these tacos.

Drain two 15-1/2-ounce cans hominy. Combine with one 4-ounce can green chilies and 1 cup sour cream. Pour into a greased baking dish. Sprinkle with cheddar cheese. Bake, uncovered, at 350° for 30 minutes.

Sweet 'n' Spicy Chicken

Prep/Total Time: 20 min.

>   1   pound boneless skinless chicken breasts,
>   cut into 1/2-inch cubes
>   3   tablespoons taco seasoning
>   1   to 2 tablespoons vegetable oil
>   1   jar (11 ounces) chunky salsa
>   1/2   cup peach preserves
> Hot cooked rice

Place the chicken in a large resealable plastic bag; add taco seasoning and toss to coat. In a skillet, brown chicken in oil. Combine salsa and preserves; stir into skillet. Bring to a boil. Reduce heat; cover and simmer for 2-3 minutes or until meat juices run clear. Serve over rice.

Yield: 4 servings.

Preparation Pointer

Sweet 'n' Spicy Chicken calls for 3 tablespoons taco seasoning. An envelope of seasoning contains 1/4 cup.

Use the remaining tablespoon to make the Soft Chicken Tacos on page 111.

Taste Twist

Apricot preserves can be used in place of the peach preserves.

Chicken Veggie Saute

Prep/Total time: 25 min.

4 boneless skinless chicken
breast halves
1 tablespoon vegetable oil
1/2 cup sliced carrots
1 cup broccoli florets
1 cup sliced fresh
mushrooms
1 can (10-3/4 ounces)
condensed cream of
chicken soup, undiluted
1/3 cup milk
1 tablespoon Dijon mustard
1/8 teaspoon pepper
Hot cooked noodles

In a large skillet, cook chicken in oil for 10 minutes or until juices
run clear. Remove and keep warm. In the drippings, saute carrots for 2 minutes. Add broccoli; saute for 2 minutes. Add mushrooms; saute for 1 minute or until vegetables are crisp-tender.

Stir in soup, milk, mustard and pepper. Bring just to a boil.
Return chicken to pan. Reduce heat; cover and simmer for 10 minutes or until heated through. Serve over noodles.

Yield: 4 servings.

Keep Chicken Juicy

When placing chicken
pieces in a pan and when
turning, use tongs or a
spatula. Piercing the
chicken with a fork allows
the juices to escape.

Cook chicken only until
it tests done. Overcooking
makes it dry.

Mustard Chicken Breasts

Prep/Total Time: 25 min.

- 4 bone-in chicken breast halves (6 ounces *each*), skin removed
- 1 teaspoon paprika
- 1 medium lemon, thinly sliced
- 1/3 cup spicy brown *or* horseradish mustard
- 1/3 cup honey
- 1 teaspoon dried minced onion
- 1/2 teaspoon curry powder
- 1/2 teaspoon lemon juice

Testing Chicken for Doneness

To check if chicken is completely cooked through, make a small slit with the tip of a knife into the thickest part of the chicken and pry the slit open.

The meat should be opaque with no signs of pink coloring. If the juices do not run clear, continue cooking.

Arrange chicken in a 9- or 10-in. microwave-safe pie plate, with the thickest side toward the outside of the plate. Sprinkle with paprika; top with lemon slices. Cover with waxed paper. Microwave on high for 8-10 minutes, rotating dish a half turn once.

In a small microwave-safe bowl, combine the remaining ingredients. Microwave, uncovered, on high for 1-1/2 to 2 minutes or until heated through; stir. Drain chicken; top with sauce. Cover and cook on high for 2 minutes or until meat juices run clear.

Editor's Note: This recipe was tested in an 850-watt microwave.

Yield: 4 servings.

Raspberry Chicken Salad

Prep/Total Time: 30 min.

  1 cup 100% raspberry spreadable fruit
1/3 cup raspberry vinegar
  4 boneless skinless chicken breast halves (4 ounces each)
  8 cups torn mixed salad greens
  1 small red onion, thinly sliced
 24 fresh raspberries

In a small bowl, combine spreadable fruit and vinegar; set aside 3/4 cup for dressing. Broil chicken 4 in. from the heat for 5-7 minutes on each side or until juices run clear, basting occasionally with remaining raspberry mixture. Cool for 10 minutes.

Meanwhile, arrange greens and onion on salad plates. Slice chicken; place over greens. Drizzle with reserved dressing. Garnish with raspberries.

Yield: 4 servings.

Berry Basics

Purchase brightly colored, plump berries without hulls. Avoid soft, shriveled or moldy berries.

   To prevent bruising when storing in the refrigerator, place raspberries in a single layer in a paper-towel-lined bowl; cover with another paper towel.

   Raspberries stay fresh in the refrigerator for up to 3 days…if you can stop your family from eating them as a snack!

Chicken Cordon Bleu in Pastry

Prep/Total Time: 30 min.

  1   tube (8 ounces) refrigerated crescent rolls
1/4   cup spreadable chive and onion cream cheese
  4   thin slices deli ham
  4   boneless skinless chicken breast halves
      (4 ounces *each*)
  4   slices Swiss cheese

On an ungreased baking sheet, separate dough into four rectangles; seal perforations. Spread 1 tablespoon cream cheese lengthwise down the center of each rectangle. Place ham widthwise over dough. Arrange chicken in center of each rectangle. Wrap ham around chicken. At each long end, pinch dough together around chicken, forming points.

Bake at 375° for 15 minutes. Top with slice of Swiss cheese; bake 5 minutes longer or until cheese is melted and pastry is golden brown.

Yield: 4 servings.

Preparation Pointers

Pick up a package of thinly sliced ham luncheon meat. You'll find several varieties, including baked, honey and smoked. Use whatever flavor you like in this recipe.

Remember to ask the person at the deli counter to thinly slice four slices of Swiss cheese.

Salsa Chicken

Prep/Total Time: 15 min.

1-1/2 pounds boneless skinless chicken breasts, cut into thin strips
1 tablespoon vegetable oil
1 medium green pepper, cut into thin strips
2 cups salsa

In a large skillet, saute chicken in oil for 3 minutes. Add the green pepper; cook for 3 minutes or until peppers are crisp-tender. Stir in salsa; bring to a boil. Reduce hear; simmer, uncovered, for 3 minutes or until chicken juices run clear.

Yield: 4 servings.

Perfect Partner

Help cool off your palate when eating spicy Salsa Chicken by offering cool fresh fruit (like honeydew melon slices) on the side.

Serving Suggestion

In addition to serving this chicken over rice, it can be used as a filling for fajitas. Don't forget the sour cream and guacamole!

Nutty Chicken Stir-Fry

   1 tablespoon cornstarch
3/4 cup orange juice
1/4 cup honey
   3 tablespoons soy sauce
1/4 teaspoon ground ginger
   2 cups sliced celery
1-1/2 cups sliced carrots
   4 teaspoons vegetable oil, *divided*
   1 pound boneless skinless chicken
      breasts, cut into 1/2-inch strips
1/4 cup coarsely chopped peanuts
Hot cooked rice, optional

In a small bowl, combine the first five ingredients until smooth; set aside. In a nonstick skillet or wok, stir-fry celery and carrots in 2 teaspoons oil until crisp-tender. Remove and keep warm. In the same skillet, stir-fry chicken in remaining oil until no longer pink.

Return vegetables to the pan. Stir orange juice mixture and add to the pan. Bring to a boil; cook and stir for 2 minutes or until thickened. Sprinkle with nuts. Serve over rice if desired.

Yield: 4 servings.

Serving Suggestions

Chopped peanuts provide a little crunch to this stir-fry. Feel free to experiment with cashews, water chestnuts and sliced celery.

Hot green tea or raspberry iced tea are delicious drinks to serve with stir-fries.

Sesame Ginger Chicken

Prep/Total Time: 25 min.

2 tablespoons soy sauce
2 tablespoons honey
1 tablespoon sesame seeds, toasted
1/2 teaspoon ground ginger
4 boneless skinless chicken breast halves
2 green onions with tops, cut into thin strips

In a small bowl, combine the first four ingredients; set aside. Pound the chicken breasts to 1/4-in. thickness. Grill over medium-hot heat, turning and basting frequently with soy sauce mixture, for 8 minutes or until juices run clear. Garnish with onions.

Yield: 4 servings.

Pleasing Partners

Round out this meaty meal with a filling side dish like a quick-cooking noodle or rice mix in teriyaki or Asian flavor.

Preparation Pointer

Toasting sesame seeds brings out their nutty flavor. Toast them in a skillet over medium heat—or in a 350° oven—stirring occasionally, just until they are golden brown.

Or pick up a bottle of toasted sesame seeds in the Oriental food aisle.

Dijon Chicken

Prep/Total Time: 25 min.

2/3 cup prepared ranch salad dressing
2 tablespoons Dijon mustard
4 boneless skinless chicken breast halves (4 ounces *each*)
1/4 cup butter
1/4 cup plus 2 tablespoons white wine *or* chicken broth
Hot cooked long grain and wild rice *or* pasta

In a small bowl, combine salad dressing and mustard; set aside. In a skillet, cook chicken in butter over medium heat for 8-10 minutes or until juices run clear. Remove and keep warm.

Add wine or broth to skillet; cook over medium heat for 2 minutes, stirring to loosen browned bits from pan. Whisk in mustard mixture; cook and stir until blended and heated through. Serve over chicken and rice. Garnish with parsley if desired.

Yield: 4 servings.

Simple Spinach Salad

Place 3 cups fresh baby spinach (about half of a 6-oz. package) in a large bowl. Toss in 1/3 cup real bacon bits and 1/4 cup crumbled blue cheese. You can also add hard-boiled egg slices if desired.

In a jar with a tight-fitting lid, combine 1/3 cup olive oil, 2 tablespoons cider vinegar, 2 teaspoons brown sugar, 1/2 teaspoon dried thyme, 1/2 teaspoon minced garlic and 1/4 teaspoon salt; shake well. Drizzle over salad and toss to coat.

Corny Chicken Wraps

Prep/Total Time: 10 min.

2 cups cubed cooked chicken breast
1 can (11 ounces) whole kernel corn, drained
1 cup salsa
1 cup (4 ounces) shredded cheddar cheese
8 flour tortillas (6 inches), warmed

In a saucepan or microwave-safe bowl, combine chicken, corn and salsa. Cook until heated through. Sprinkle cheese over tortillas. Place about 1/2 cup chicken mixture down the center of each tortilla; roll up. Secure with toothpicks.

Yield: 4 servings.

Salsa Versus Picante

What's the difference between salsa and picante?

Typically, salsa is thinner with larger chunks of vegetables.

Picante is thicker and smoother with smaller pieces of vegetables. They are usually interchangeable in recipes.

Enchilada Chicken Soup

Prep/Total Time: 10 min.

  1 can (11 ounces) condensed fiesta nacho cheese
     soup, undiluted
  1 can (10-3/4 ounces) condensed cream of chicken
     soup, undiluted
2-2/3 cups milk
  1 can (10 ounces) chunk white chicken, drained
  1 can (10 ounces) enchilada sauce
  1 can (4 ounces) chopped green chilies
Sour cream

In a large saucepan, combine the soups, milk, chicken, enchilada sauce and chilies; mix well. Cook until heated through. Garnish with sour cream.

Yield: 7 servings.

Chicken in Creamy Gravy

Prep/Total Time: 25 min.

4 boneless skinless chicken breast halves (1 pound)
1 tablespoon vegetable oil
1 can (10-3/4 ounces) condensed cream of chicken and broccoli soup, undiluted
1/4 cup milk
2 teaspoons lemon juice
1/8 teaspoon pepper
4 lemon slices

In a nonstick skillet, cook chicken in oil until browned on both sides, about 10 minutes; drain. In a bowl, combine soup, milk, lemon juice and pepper. Pour over chicken. Top each chicken breast with a lemon slice. Reduce heat; cover and simmer until chicken juices run clear, about 5 minutes.

Yield: 4 servings.

Good Gravy!

Cut the fat and calories in Chicken in Creamy Gravy by using reduced-fat soup and fat-free milk.

Or if you're not watching your waistline, replacing the milk with half-and-half cream will yield a richer, creamier gravy.

Pineapple Chicken Stir-Fry

Prep/Total Time: 25 min.

1 can (20 ounces) unsweetened
   pineapple tidbits
2 tablespoons cornstarch
1/4 cup cider vinegar
1/4 cup ketchup
2 tablespoons brown sugar
2 tablespoons soy sauce
1/4 teaspoon ground ginger
1-1/2 pounds boneless skinless chicken
   breasts, cubed
3 tablespoons vegetable oil,
   divided
1/2 teaspoon garlic salt
2 medium carrots, sliced
1 medium green pepper, julienned
1 medium tomato, cut into wedges
Hot cooked rice

Drain pineapple, reserving the juice; set pineapple aside. In a small bowl, combine cornstarch and reserved juice until smooth. Stir in vinegar, ketchup, brown sugar, soy sauce and ginger; set aside.

In a wok or large skillet, stir-fry the chicken in 2 tablespoons oil for 5-6 minutes or until juices run clear; sprinkle with garlic salt. Remove and keep warm. Stir-fry the carrots in remaining oil for 4 minutes. Add green pepper; cook and stir until vegetables are crisp-tender. Add the chicken and pineapple.

Stir pineapple juice mixture; pour into pan. Bring to a boil; cook and stir for 1-2 minutes or until thickened. Add the tomato wedges. Serve over rice.

Yield: 6 servings.

Preparation Pointer

When adding the pineapple juice mixture, push the ingredients up to the side of the wok and form a well in the middle. Add the sauce in the middle and stir to thicken before mixing with the other ingredients.

Serving Suggestion

For even more flavor, add some onion wedges to this dish.

Potato Chip Chicken

Prep/Total Time: 15 min.

- 1 cup coarsely crushed potato chips
- 1 tablespoon minced fresh parsley
- 1/2 teaspoon salt
- 1/2 teaspoon paprika
- 1/4 teaspoon onion powder
- 4 boneless skinless chicken breast halves (about 1 pound)
- 2 tablespoons mayonnaise

In a large resealable plastic bag, combine the potato chips, parsley, salt, paprika and onion powder. Brush chicken with mayonnaise; add chicken to the crumb mixture and shake to coat.

Place in an ungreased microwave-safe 11-in. x 7-in. x 2-in. baking dish. Cover with microwave-safe paper towels; cook on high for 8-10 minutes or until chicken juices run clear.

Editor's Note: This recipe was tested in an 850-watt microwave.

Yield: 4 servings.

Chip Choices

Looking for a use for the crumbs of the potato chip bag that no one seems to eat? Make Potato Chip Chicken!

A single flavor (like regular, sour cream and onion, barbecue or cheddar cheese)—or a combination of flavors—can be used.

Basil Brussels Sprouts (p. 270)

From down-home dinners to more elegant entrees, turkey solves any dining dilemma.

Turkey Pasta Supreme (p. 145)

Timeless **Turkey**

Turkey in a Pot (p. 143)

Spicy Kielbasa Soup
(p. 147)

In-a-Hurry Turkey

Prep/Total Time: 25 min.

>   2 turkey tenderloins
>   (1-1/2 pounds)
>   1/4 cup butter
>   3/4 teaspoon dried thyme
>   1/2 teaspoon dried rosemary,
>   crushed
>   1/4 teaspoon paprika
>   1/8 teaspoon garlic powder

Cut tenderloins in half lengthwise, then into serving-size pieces. Place on the rack of a broiler pan. In a small saucepan, heat the remaining ingredients until butter is melted.

Broil turkey until lightly browned on one side. Brush with the herb butter; turn and brown the other side. Brush with butter. Continue cooking 6-8 minutes or until no longer pink, brushing often with butter.

Yield: 6 servings.

Crushed Rosemary

To release the flavor of dried rosemary, crush it in the palm of your hand.

Or place the measured amount of rosemary leaves in a resealable plastic bag; seal. Use a rolling pin to crush the leaves.

Berry Turkey Sandwich

Prep/Total Time: 5 min.

>   4 slices whole wheat bread
>   2 lettuce leaves
>   2 slices Swiss cheese
>   1/4 pound thinly sliced deli turkey breast
>   4 fresh strawberries, sliced
>   2 tablespoons whipped cream cheese spread
>   2 teaspoons finely chopped pecans

On two slices of bread, layer the lettuce, cheese, turkey and strawberries. Combine cream cheese and pecans; spread over remaining bread. Place over strawberries. Serve immediately.

Yield: 2 servings.

Preparation Pointer

Buy a small bag of finely chopped pecans and use 2 teaspoons in this recipe.

Put the remaining nuts in a resealable plastic bag and store in the freezer. Use the leftovers to make Nut-Crusted Fried Fish (p. 239) or to sprinkle over ice cream.

Substitution Idea

Oatmeal, sourdough and sunflower seed bread can be used in place of the whole wheat bread in this recipe.

Tarragon Turkey Patties

Prep/Total Time: 20 min.

1 cup crushed corn bread
   stuffing
2 large eggs
2 tablespoons minced fresh
   tarragon
1/2 teaspoon pepper
1 pound lean ground turkey

TARRAGON-MUSTARD SAUCE:

2 cups chicken broth
1/4 cup minced fresh tarragon
3 teaspoons Dijon mustard

In a bowl, combine the stuffing, eggs, tarragon and pepper. Crumble turkey over mixture and mix well. Shape into four patties. In a non-stick skillet coated with nonstick cooking spray, cook patties over medium heat for 4 minutes on each side or until juices run clear and a meat thermometer reads 165°. Remove and keep warm.

For sauce, add the broth, tarragon and mustard to the skillet; bring to a boil. Reduce heat; simmer, uncovered, for 5 minutes or until reduced by three-fourths. Serve with turkey patties.

Yield: 4 servings.

Tarragon Tips

When buying tarragon, it should have a firm stem, nice straight leaves without blackening or yellowing, and it shouldn't be wilting.

The strength of its essential oil means that it keeps better than other herbs.

Store tarragon in a plastic bag in the refrigerator crisper drawer, or place the stems in a glass of water.

Turkey Noodle Stew

Prep/Total Time: 30 min.

2 turkey breast tenderloins (about 1/2 pound *each*),
   cut into 1/4-inch slices
1 medium onion, chopped
1 tablespoon vegetable oil
1 can (14-1/2 ounces) chicken broth
1 can (10-3/4 ounces) condensed cream of celery
   soup, undiluted
2 cups frozen mixed vegetables
1/2 to 1 teaspoon lemon-pepper seasoning
3 cups uncooked extra-wide egg noodles

In a large skillet, cook turkey and onion in oil until turkey is no longer pink, about 6 minutes; drain. Combine the broth, soup, vegetables and lemon-pepper. Add to the skillet; bring to a boil. Stir in noodles. Reduce heat; cover and simmer for 10 minutes or until noodles and vegetables are tender.

Yield: 6 servings.

Quick Complement

Convenient refrigerated biscuits get a tasty treatment when topped with crushed corn chips.

   Separate 1 tube (7-1/2 ounces) refrigerated home-style biscuits into 10 biscuits; arrange in a greased 8-in. round baking pan. Brush with 1 tablespoon melted butter. Sprinkle with 1/3 cup crushed corn chips; gently press into the dough. Bake at 400° for 14-16 minutes or until golden brown.

Substitution Secret

Can't find turkey breast tenderloins? Turkey breast slices or strips can be used instead.

Tomato-Turkey Pasta Sauce

Prep/Total Time: 20 min.

- 1 **pound turkey Italian sausage links, casings removed**
- 1/2 **cup chopped green onions**
- 2 **garlic cloves, minced**
- 2 **teaspoons olive oil**
- 2 **cans (14-1/2 ounces** *each***) diced tomatoes, undrained**
- 1/2 **cup white wine** *or* **chicken broth**
- 1 **cup loosely packed fresh basil, minced**
- 1 **teaspoon dried oregano**

Hot cooked spaghetti
- 1/2 **cup shredded Parmesan cheese**

In a large nonstick skillet, cook the sausage, onions and garlic in oil over medium heat until sausage is no longer pink; drain. Add the tomatoes, wine or broth, basil and oregano; bring to a boil. Reduce heat; simmer, uncovered, for 10 minutes or until heated through. Serve over spaghetti; sprinkle with Parmesan.

Yield: 8 servings.

Pasta Pointer

To save a little time, buy fresh pasta from the dairy section—it cooks more quickly than dried pasta.

Simple Salad

While the pasta sauce is simmering, open a bagged salad kit, toss in some cucumber slices and grape tomatoes. Drizzle with dressing and toss to coat.

Lemony Turkey Breast

Prep: 10 min.   **Cook:** 5 hours

1   **bone-in turkey breast
(5 pounds), halved**
1   **medium lemon, halved**
1   **teaspoon lemon-pepper
seasoning**
1   **teaspoon garlic salt**
4   **teaspoons cornstarch**
1/2 **cup chicken broth**

Remove skin from turkey. Pat turkey dry with paper towels; spray turkey with non-stick cooking spray. Place breast side up in a slow cooker. Squeeze half of the lemon over turkey; sprinkle with lemon-pepper and garlic salt. Place lemon halves under turkey. Cover and cook on low for 5-7 hours or until meat is no longer pink and a meat thermometer reads 170°. Remove turkey and keep warm. Discard lemon.

For gravy, pour cooking liquid into a measuring cup; skim fat. In a saucepan, combine cornstarch and broth until smooth. Gradually stir in cooking liquid. Bring to a boil; cook and stir for 2 minutes or until thickened. Serve with turkey.

Yield: 14 servings.

Lively Leftovers

This entree makes a lot, so make the most of the leftovers.

Extra cooked turkey can be stored in the refrigerator for 1-2 days or in the freezer for up to 3 months.

Use it to make a variety of dishes in this chapter, including Turkey Nachos (p. 141), Cranberry-Chutney Turkey Salad (p. 148) and Asparagus-Turkey Pasta Toss (p. 152).

Cranberry Turkey Cutlets

Prep/Total Time: 30 min.

> 1 cup thinly sliced onion
> 2 teaspoons vegetable oil
> 2 cups dried cranberries
> 2 cups orange juice
> 1-1/2 teaspoons balsamic vinegar
> 6 turkey cutlets (4 ounces *each* and 1/2 inch thick)
> 1/2 teaspoon salt
> 1/2 teaspoon pepper

In a large skillet, saute onion in oil until lightly browned, about 6 minutes. Stir in the cranberries, orange juice and vinegar. Bring to a boil over medium heat; cook and stir until sauce begins to thicken. Set aside.

Coat grill rack with nonstick cooking spray before starting the grill. Sprinkle turkey cutlets with salt and pepper. Grill, covered, over indirect medium heat for 5-6 minutes on each side or until juices run clear. Top each cutlet with some of the cranberry sauce; grill 1-2 minutes longer. Serve with remaining cranberry sauce.

Yield: 6 servings.

Turkey Cutlet Tip

Turkey cutlets are small, thin steaks that are removed from the breast meat and are pounded to flatten and tenderize them. Turkey cutlets are available uncooked or fully cooked, unbreaded or breaded, and unflavored or seasoned with various herbs and spices.

They can be used as a substitute in recipes calling for beef, veal, or pork cutlets.

Turkey Stir-Fry

Prep/Total Time: 20 min.

2 tablespoons sugar
1 tablespoon cornstarch
3 tablespoons water
3 tablespoons soy sauce
1 cup fresh *or* frozen snow peas
1 medium sweet red pepper, cut into chunks
10 large fresh mushrooms, quartered
2 tablespoons vegetable oil
2 cups cubed cooked turkey
Hot cooked rice

In a bowl, combine the sugar and cornstarch. Stir in water and soy sauce until smooth; set aside. In a skillet, saute the peas, red pepper and mushrooms in oil until tender. Add the turkey and soy sauce mixture. Bring to a boil; cook and stir for 2 minutes or until thickened. Serve over rice.

Yield: 6 servings.

Substitution Secret

If you don't have any cooked turkey on hand, stop by the deli to pick up a large piece of turkey breast. Then take it home to cut up.

Or you can make Turkey Stir-Fry with fresh turkey tenderloin strips. Just be sure to adjust the cooking time so the turkey is cooked through.

Turkey Enchiladas

Prep: 10 min.   **Cook:** 6 hours

    2 turkey thighs *or* drumsticks
       (about 2 pounds)
    1 can (8 ounces) tomato sauce
    1 can (4 ounces) chopped
       green chilies
  1/3 cup chopped onion
    2 tablespoons Worcestershire
       sauce
    1 to 2 tablespoons chili powder
  1/4 teaspoon garlic powder
    8 flour tortillas (6 inches)
Optional toppings: chopped green
   onions, sliced ripe olives, chopped
   tomatoes, shredded cheddar
   cheese, sour cream *and/or*
   shredded lettuce

Remove skin from turkey. Place in a 5-qt. slow cooker. Combine tomato sauce, chilies, onion, Worcestershire sauce, chili powder and garlic powder; pour over turkey. Cover and cook on low for 6-8 hours or until turkey is tender. Remove turkey; shred meat with a fork and return to the slow cooker. Heat through.

Spoon about 1/2 cup of turkey mixture down the center of each tortilla. Fold bottom of tortilla over filling and roll up. Add toppings of your choice.

Yield: 4 servings.

Serving Suggestion

Complete this Mexican meal with a speedy side of Spanish rice.

In a saucepan over medium heat, bring 1-1/2 cups water, 1 cup salsa and 2 chicken bouillon cubes to a boil. Stir in 2 cups uncooked instant rice; remove from the heat. Cover and let stand 6-8 minutes or until liquid is absorbed. Fluff with a fork.

Brown Rice Turkey Soup

Prep/Total Time: 30 min.

1 cup diced sweet red pepper
1/2 cup chopped onion
1/2 cup sliced celery
2 garlic cloves, minced
2 tablespoons butter
3 cans (14-1/2 ounces *each*) chicken broth
3/4 cup white wine *or* additional chicken broth
1 teaspoon dried thyme
1/4 teaspoon pepper
2 cups cubed cooked turkey breast
1 cup instant brown rice
1/4 cup sliced green onions

About Brown Rice

Rice from which only the hull has been removed is called brown rice. When cooked, it has a slightly chewy texture and a nut-like flavor. Brown rice is a natural source of bran.

Because of the oil content in the bran, brown rice has a shelf life of about 6 months and keeps best when refrigerated.

In a Dutch oven, saute red pepper, onion, celery and garlic in butter for 5-7 minutes or until vegetables are tender. Add broth, wine or additional broth, thyme and pepper. Bring to a boil. Reduce heat; cover and simmer for 5 minutes.

Stir in turkey and rice. Bring to a boil; simmer, uncovered, for 5 minutes or until rice is tender. Garnish with green onions.

Yield: 5 servings.

Tasty Turkey Skillet

Prep/Total Time: 30 min.

1 pound turkey breast tenderloins, cut into 1/4-inch strips
1 package (5.3 ounces) Oriental fried rice mix
1 tablespoon butter
2 cups water
1/8 teaspoon cayenne pepper
1-1/2 cups frozen corn, thawed
1 cup frozen broccoli cuts, thawed
2 tablespoons chopped sweet red pepper, optional

In a nonstick skillet coated with nonstick cooking spray, saute turkey until no longer pink; drain. Remove turkey and keep warm. Set aside seasoning packet from rice. In the skillet, saute rice in butter until lightly browned. Stir in the water, cayenne and contents of seasoning packet.

Bring to a boil. Reduce heat; cover and simmer for 15 minutes. Stir in corn, broccoli, red pepper if desired and turkey. Return to a boil. Reduce heat; cover and simmer for 6-8 minutes or until the rice and vegetables are tender.

Yield: 4-6 servings.

Substitution Secret

Feel free to replace the frozen corn and broccoli with your favorite frozen mixed vegetables.

Timely Tip

If you use a pound of cubed cooked turkey, you can skip the first step in the recipe …and save a bit of time!

Pizza on a Stick

Prep/Total Time: 30 min.

8 ounces turkey Italian sausage links
2 cups whole fresh mushrooms
2 cups cherry tomatoes
1 medium onion, cut into 1-inch pieces
1 large green pepper, cut into 1-inch pieces
30 slices turkey pepperoni (2 ounces)
1 tube (10 ounces) refrigerated pizza crust
1-1/2 cups (6 ounces) shredded mozzarella cheese
1-1/4 cups pizza sauce, warmed

In a large nonstick skillet, cook the sausage over medium heat until no longer pink; drain. When cool enough to handle, cut sausage into 20 pieces. On 10 metal or soaked wooden skewers, alternately thread the sausage, vegetables and pepperoni.

Unroll the pizza dough onto a lightly floured surface; cut widthwise into 1-in.-wide strips. Starting at the pointed end of a prepared skewer, pierce skewer through one end of dough strip and press dough against last ingredients on the skewer. Spiral-wrap dough strip around skewer, allowing vegetables and meats to peek through. Wrap the remaining end of dough strip around skewer above the first ingredient. Repeat with remaining dough strips and prepared skewers.

Arrange kabobs on a baking sheet coated with nonstick cooking spray. Bake at 400° for 10-12 minutes or until vegetables are tender and pizza crust is golden. Immediately sprinkle with cheese. Serve with pizza sauce.

Yield: 5 servings.

Do-Ahead Idea

The instructions for Pizza on a Stick may seem long, but much of the preparation can be done the night before.

Cook the turkey sausage links and slice. Make the sausage, vegetable and pepperoni kabobs. Cover and refrigerate.

The next day, just wrap the strips of pizza dough around the kabobs and bake as directed.

Smoked Sausage with Pasta

Prep/Total Time: 25 min.

    4   ounces uncooked
        angel hair pasta
  1/2   pound smoked turkey
        sausage, cut into 1/2-inch
        slices
    2   cups sliced fresh
        mushrooms
    2   garlic cloves, minced
4-1/2   teaspoons minced fresh
        basil *or* 1-1/2 teaspoons
        dried basil
    1   tablespoon olive oil
    2   cups julienned seeded
        plum tomatoes
  1/8   teaspoon salt
  1/8   teaspoon pepper

Cook pasta according to package directions. Meanwhile, in a large nonstick skillet, saute the sausage, mushrooms, garlic and basil in oil until mushrooms are tender. Drain pasta; add to the sausage mixture. Add the tomatoes, salt and pepper; toss gently. Heat through.

Yield: 4 servings.

Tomato Tip

Plum tomatoes are often called Roma tomatoes. In general, they are meatier and less juicy than slicing tomatoes and are ideal for making sauces and for adding to other cooked foods.

Tomatoes should be stored at room temperature. Wash gently in cold water before using.

Turkey Nachos

Prep/Total Time: 10 min.

    1 **can (10-3/4 ounces) condensed cheddar cheese soup, undiluted**
3/4 **cup salsa**
    1 **cup cubed cooked turkey**
Tortilla chips

Combine the soup and salsa in a saucepan or microwave-safe bowl. Stir in the turkey; cook until heated through. Serve warm with tortilla chips.

Yield: about 2 cups.

Mexican Fiesta!

Turkey Nachos can be part of a mouth-watering Mexican buffet!

Have both crispy corn taco shells and soft flour tortillas warmed and on hand.

Then, let your guests choose from a variety of fillings, such as shredded beef, pork or chicken.

Offer tasty toppings, like refried beans, shredded lettuce, diced tomatoes, sliced green onions, sliced ripe olives, shredded cheese and, of course, salsa!

Teen Tastes

When your teenagers ask friends to stay for dinner, whip up this thick, cheesy turkey dip.

The recipe can easily be doubled or tripled, especially if you keep packs of cubed cooked turkey in the freezer and the rest of the ingredients in the pantry.

Vegetable Turkey Skillet

Prep/Total Time: 20 min.

1   pound ground turkey breast
1   small onion, chopped
1   garlic clove, minced
1   teaspoon vegetable oil
1   pound fresh tomatoes, chopped
1/4   pound zucchini, diced
1/4   cup chopped dill pickle
1   teaspoon dried basil
1/2   teaspoon pepper

In a skillet, brown turkey, onion and garlic in oil. Add remaining ingredients. Simmer, uncovered, for 5-10 minutes or until the turkey is cooked and zucchini is tender.

Yield: 6 servings.

Substitution Secret

One pound of fresh tomatoes will yield about 1-1/2 cups chopped.

For faster preparation, substitute the fresh tomatoes in this recipe with one 14-1/2-ounce can of diced, drained tomatoes.

Turkey in a Pot

Prep: 25 min.   **Cook:** 5 hours

1   boneless turkey breast
     (3 to 4 pounds), halved
1   can (16 ounces) whole-berry
     cranberry sauce
1/2 cup sugar
1/2 cup apple juice
1   tablespoon cider vinegar
2   garlic cloves, minced
1   teaspoon ground mustard
1/2 teaspoon ground cinnamon
1/4 teaspoon ground cloves
1/4 teaspoon ground allspice
2   tablespoons all-purpose
     flour
1/4 cup cold water
1/4 teaspoon browning sauce, optional

Place the turkey skin side up in a 5-qt. slow cooker. Combine the cranberry sauce, sugar, apple juice, vinegar, garlic, mustard, cinnamon, cloves and allspice; pour over turkey. Cover and cook on low for 5-6 hours or until a meat thermometer reads 170°.

Remove turkey to a cutting board; keep warm. Strain cooking juices. In a saucepan, combine flour and water until smooth; gradually stir in strained juices. Bring to a boil; cook and stir for 2 minutes or until thickened. Stir in browning sauce if desired. Serve with sliced turkey.

Yield: 12-16 servings.

Browning Sauce Secret

Because a slow cooker won't brown the turkey and drippings, you may want to add a bit of browning sauce to the gravy.

Preparation Pointer

Treat your family to a turkey dinner during the week by serving Turkey in a Pot, which gets a "holiday" treatment with cranberry gravy.

Round out the meal with a frozen vegetable and stuffing mix.

Breaded Turkey Breasts

Prep/Total Time: 20 min.

- 1 cup dry bread crumbs
- 1/4 cup grated Parmesan cheese
- 2 teaspoons Italian seasoning
- 1 cup milk
- 1 pound boneless skinless turkey breast slices
- 1/4 cup olive oil

In a shallow bowl, combine the bread crumbs, Parmesan cheese and Italian seasoning. Pour milk into another shallow bowl. Dip turkey in milk, then in the crumb mixture.

In a large skillet over medium heat, cook turkey in oil for 8-10 minutes or until juices run clear. Drain on paper towels.

Yield: 4 servings.

Preparation Pointer

For an even heartier coating, dip the turkey slices in a beaten egg instead of milk.

Time-Saving Tip

Seasoned bread crumbs can be used in place of the dry bread crumbs and Italian seasoning.

Turkey Pasta Supreme

Prep/Total Time: 20 min.

3/4	pound uncooked turkey breast
2	garlic cloves, minced
2	tablespoons butter
1-1/4	cups heavy whipping cream
2	tablespoons minced fresh basil *or* 2 teaspoons dried basil
1/4	cup grated Parmesan cheese

Dash pepper

3	to 4 cups hot cooked pasta

Cut turkey into 2-in. x 1/4-in. pieces. In a skillet, saute turkey and garlic in butter until turkey is browned and no longer pink, about 6 minutes. Add cream, basil, Parmesan and pepper; bring to a boil. Reduce heat; simmer for 3 minutes, stirring frequently. Stir in pasta and toss to coat.

Yield: 4 servings.

Easy Minced Garlic

If you don't want to mess with mincing fresh garlic, keep a jar of minced garlic in the refrigerator. One fresh minced garlic clove is equal to 1/2 teaspoon bottled minced garlic.

Pasta Pointer

For 3 to 4 cups of cooked penne pasta, start with about 8 ounces dry pasta.

Fiesta Fry Pan Dinner

Prep/Total Time: 30 min.

1   pound ground turkey
1/2   cup chopped onion
1   envelope taco seasoning
1-1/2   cups water
1-1/2   cups sliced zucchini
1   can (14-1/2 ounces) stewed tomatoes, undrained
1   cup frozen corn
1-1/2   cups uncooked instant rice
1   cup (4 ounces) shredded cheddar cheese

In a skillet, cook turkey and onion until meat is no longer pink; drain if necessary. Stir in taco seasoning, water, zucchini, tomatoes and corn; bring to a boil. Add rice. Reduce heat; cover and simmer for 5 minutes or until rice is tender and liquid is absorbed. Sprinkle with cheese; cover and let stand until the cheese is melted.

Yield: 8-10 servings.

Zucchini Secrets

Look for zucchini with glossy, smooth and firm but tender skins. Place unwashed in a sealed plastic bag and store in the refrigerator crisper drawer for up to 4 days. Before using, wash and cut off stem and blossom ends.

A half pound of zucchini will yield about 1-1/2 cups sliced.

Spicy Kielbasa Soup

Prep: 15 min. **Cook:** 8 hours

- 1/2 pound smoked turkey kielbasa, sliced
- 1 medium onion, chopped
- 1 medium green pepper, chopped
- 1 celery rib with leaves, thinly sliced
- 4 garlic cloves, minced
- 2 cans (14-1/2 ounces *each*) chicken broth
- 1 can (15-1/2 ounces) great northern beans, rinsed and drained
- 1 can (14-1/2 ounces) stewed tomatoes, cut up
- 1 small zucchini, sliced
- 1 medium carrot, shredded
- 1 tablespoon dried parsley flakes
- 1/4 teaspoon crushed red pepper flakes
- 1/4 teaspoon pepper

In a nonstick skillet, cook kielbasa over medium heat until lightly browned. Add the onion, green pepper, celery and garlic. Cook and stir for 5 minutes or until vegetable are tender. Transfer to a slow cooker. Stir in the remaining ingredients. Cover and cook on low for 8-9 hours.

Yield: 5 servings.

Preparation Pointer

Leftovers of this zippy soup make great leftovers. So you may want to double the recipe and reheat for dinner the next night.

Serving Suggestion

Fresh rye bread with butter is all you need to pair with this soup with old-world flavor.

Cranberry-Chutney Turkey Salad

Prep/Total Time: 15 min.

3 cups diced cooked turkey breast
1/2 cup dried cranberries
1/3 cup chopped pecans
1/3 cup diced onion
1/3 cup diced green pepper
1/2 cup mayonnaise
1/2 cup sour cream
1 tablespoon lemon juice
1/2 teaspoon ground ginger
1/8 teaspoon cayenne pepper
Leaf lettuce, optional

In a large bowl, combine the turkey, cranberries, pecans, onion and green pepper. In a small bowl, combine the mayonnaise, sour cream, lemon juice, ginger and cayenne. Pour over turkey mixture; stir gently to coat. Cover and refrigerate until serving. Serve in a lettuce-lined bowl if desired.

Yield: 6 servings.

Serving Suggestion

Try serving Cranberry-Chutney Turkey Salad as a sandwich.

Spoon on top of slices of your favorite bread. Or use it as a filling for white or whole wheat pita pockets.

Super Sloppy Joes

Prep/Total Time: 25 min.

1	pound ground turkey breast
1/4	cup chopped onion
1/2	cup ketchup
3	tablespoons barbecue sauce
1	tablespoon prepared mustard
1	tablespoon vinegar
1-1/2	teaspoons Worcestershire sauce
1/2	teaspoon celery seed
1/4	teaspoon pepper
6	whole wheat hamburger buns, split

In a nonstick skillet, cook the turkey and onion for 5 minutes or until turkey is no longer pink. Add the next seven ingredients; simmer for 10 minutes, stirring occasionally. Serve on buns.

Yield: 6 servings.

Fast Fries

French fries are a natural to pair with sandwiches. These seasoned fries will disappear from the plate!

Place 6 cups frozen shoestring potatoes on a foil-lined baking sheet. Bake at 450° for 8 minutes.

Combine 1/2 cup grated Parmesan cheese, 2 teaspoons Italian seasoning and 1/2 teaspoon salt. Sprinkle over potatoes; mix gently.

Bake 4-5 minutes more or until the potatoes are browned and crisp.

Broiled Turkey Tenderloins

Prep/Total Time: 20 min.

3/4 cup orange juice concentrate
1/3 cup molasses
1/4 cup ketchup
  3 tablespoons prepared mustard
  2 tablespoons soy sauce
1/2 teaspoon garlic powder
1/4 teaspoon cayenne pepper
1/8 teaspoon ground cumin
  3 turkey breast tenderloins (about 1-1/2 pounds),
     cut lengthwise in half

In a saucepan, whisk the first eight ingredients; bring to a boil. Set aside 3/4 cup for serving. Brush tenderloins on both sides with remaining sauce. Broil 6 in. from the heat for 5 minutes, basting once. Turn and broil 5-8 minutes longer or until juices run clear. Serve with the reserved sauce.

Yield: 6 servings.

Basic Green Beans

A side dish of green beans nicely complements zesty Broiled Turkey Tenderloins.

Place 1 pound of fresh or frozen green beans in a saucepan and cover with water. Bring to a boil; cook until tender.

Drain all but 2 teaspoons of the liquid. Add 1 teaspoon butter and 1/2 teaspoon dill weed; stir to coat.

Cabbage Turkey Stew

Prep/Total Time: 25 min.

- 1 pound ground turkey
- 1 medium onion, chopped
- 3 garlic cloves, minced
- 4 cups chopped cabbage
- 2 medium carrots, sliced
- 1 can (28 ounces) diced
  tomatoes, undrained
- 3/4 cup water
- 1 tablespoon brown sugar
- 1 tablespoon white vinegar
- 1 teaspoon salt
- 1 teaspoon dried oregano
- 1/4 teaspoon dried thyme
- 1/4 teaspoon pepper

In a large saucepan, cook turkey, onion and garlic over medium heat until meat is no longer pink; drain. Add the remaining ingredients. Bring to a boil; cover and simmer for 6-8 minutes or until the vegetables are tender.

Yield: 6 servings.

Shredding Cabbage

To shred a head of cabbage, first cut the head through the core into quarters. Place a quarter section cut side down on a cutting board.

With a chef's knife, slice the cabbage wedge into long shreds. For chopped cabbage, coarsely chop the long shreds.

Asparagus-Turkey Pasta Toss

Prep/ Total Time: 25 min.

- 8 ounces uncooked angel hair pasta
- 2 tablespoons butter
- 2 tablespoons all-purpose flour
- 1 teaspoon chicken bouillon granules
- 1/2 teaspoon pepper
- 1/4 teaspoon salt
- 1-1/2 cups milk
- 1/2 cup shredded Swiss cheese
- 1/4 cup plus 2 tablespoons shredded Parmesan cheese
- 2 cups diced cooked turkey
- 20 fresh asparagus spears, cut into 1-inch pieces
- 1 cup sliced fresh mushrooms

Cook pasta according to package directions. In a saucepan, melt butter. Stir in the flour, bouillon, pepper and salt until smooth; gradually add milk. Bring to a boil; cook and stir 2 minutes or until thickened. Reduce heat; add cheeses and stir until smooth. Stir in the turkey, asparagus and mushrooms. Cook until heated through.

Drain pasta and place in a serving bowl. Pour sauce mixture over pasta; toss gently to coat.

Yield: 4 servings.

Asparagus Tips

Look for asparagus spears with tightly closed, compact tips. Stalks should have bright green color, while the tips may have a slight lavender tint. For more even cooking, the spears should all be about the same size and thickness.

Keep unwashed asparagus in a sealed plastic bag in the crisper drawer for up to 4 days. Soak in cold water to clean. Snap off the stalk ends.

One pound equals about 16 to 20 spears.

Smoked Sausage Stir-Fry

Prep/Total Time: 25 min.

1 pound fully cooked smoked
turkey sausage, cut into
1/2-inch slices
2 tablespoons olive oil
1/2 cup julienned green pepper
1/2 cup julienned sweet red pepper
1 small onion, sliced and
separated into rings
1-1/2 teaspoons garlic powder
1-1/2 teaspoons dried basil
1-1/2 teaspoons dried oregano
1/4 teaspoon pepper
2 medium tomatoes, cut into
wedges
4 cups hot cooked rice

In a nonstick skillet or wok, stir-fry sausage in oil over medium heat until lightly browned, about 10 minutes. Add the peppers, onion and seasonings. Cover and cook for 10 minutes or until the vegetables are crisp-tender, stirring occasionally. Add the tomatoes; cook 1 minute longer. Serve over rice.

Yield: 4 servings.

Speedy Side Dish

Your family's favorite instant rice is all you need to round out this satisfying stir-fry.

It's the perfect accompaniment to a variety of weekday dinners because it cooks in mere minutes.

Liven up ordinary weekday dinners with a selection of prime pork cuts, such as chops, ribs, tenderloin, ham and sausage.

Slow Cooker Cranberry Pork (p. 182)

Pleasing Pork

Tender 'n' Tangy Ribs (p. 195)

Aloha Pork Chops

Prep/Total Time: 20 min.

4 boneless pork loin chops
(3/4 inch thick)

1 tablespoon lemon-pepper seasoning

1 teaspoon plus 2 tablespoons olive oil, *divided*

1 cup sweet-and-sour sauce

1 can (20 ounces) pineapple chunks, drained

1/2 medium green pepper, julienned

1/2 cup chopped red onion

6 cups cold cooked rice

1/4 cup stir-fry sauce

Sprinkle pork chops with lemon-pepper. In a large skillet, brown chops on both sides in 1 teaspoon oil over medium-high heat; remove and set aside. Drain skillet; add sweet-and-sour sauce and pineapple chunks. Bring to a boil. Reduce heat; return chops to skillet. Simmer, uncovered, for 5 minutes or until meat juices run clear.

Meanwhile, in another skillet, saute the green pepper and onion in remaining oil for 2 minutes. Add rice and stir-fry sauce; cook and stir for 4 minutes or until lightly browned. Transfer to a serving platter; top with pork mixture.

Yield: 4 servings.

Cooling Rice

To quickly cool rice, spread out the cooked rice on a large baking pan or cookie sheet. Refrigerate it for 15-20 minutes or until cool.

Preparation Pointer

You'll find stir-fry sauce near the other Oriental cooking ingredients.

Peppy Parmesan Pasta

Prep/Total Time: 10 min.

- 8 ounces angel hair pasta
- 1 large tomato, chopped
- 1 package (3 ounces) sliced pepperoni
- 1 can (2-1/4 ounces) sliced ripe olives, drained
- 1/4 cup grated Parmesan cheese
- 3 tablespoons olive oil
- 1/2 teaspoon salt
- 1/4 teaspoon garlic powder

Cook pasta according to package directions. Meanwhile, in a serving bowl, combine the tomato, pepperoni, olives, Parmesan cheese, oil, salt and garlic powder. Drain pasta; add to the tomato mixture and toss to coat.

Yield: 4 servings.

Angel Hair in a Hurry

Angel hair pasta cooks faster than other varieties of pasta so you can get dinner on the table in no time. Serve this skillet dish with additional grated Parmesan cheese.

Pass the Pudding!

While you're preparing the pasta dish, have the kids make some instant pudding. It can chill while you're enjoying dinner.

Broccoli Ham Stroganoff

Prep/Total Time: 30 min.

2 cups frozen chopped broccoli
1 tablespoon water
1 tablespoon butter
1/4 cup chopped onion
3 tablespoons all-purpose flour
1 can (10-1/2 ounces) chicken broth
2 cups cubed fully cooked ham
1 cup (8 ounces) sour cream
1 jar (4-1/2 ounces) sliced mushrooms, drained
Hot cooked noodles

Place the broccoli and water in a 1-qt. microwave-safe bowl. Cover and microwave on high for 3-5 minutes or until the broccoli is tender, stirring once. Drain; set aside and keep warm.

In another microwave-safe bowl, heat butter, uncovered, on high for 20 seconds or until melted. Add onion; cover and microwave on high for 2 minutes or until tender. Stir in flour until blended. Gradually stir in broth; mix well. Microwave, uncovered, on high for 4-6 minutes or until thickened and bubbly, stirring once.

Add the ham, sour cream, mushrooms and reserved broccoli; mix well. Cook, uncovered, on high for 3-5 minutes or until heated through, stirring once. Serve over noodles.

Editor's Note: This recipe was tested in an 850-watt microwave.

Yield: 4 servings.

Broccoli Benefits

Broccoli is a nutritional powerhouse packed with Vitamins A and C, folic acid, calcium, potassium and fiber.

One 10-oz. package yields about 3 cups chopped.

Serving Suggestion

Broccoli Ham Stroganoff can also be served over toast points and over baked puff pastry shells or refrigerated biscuits.

Glazed Pork Tenderloin

Prep/Total Time: 30 min.

1/4   teaspoon salt
1/4   teaspoon pepper
   1   pork tenderloin (1 pound)
   2   sprigs fresh rosemary
1/2   cup pineapple preserves
   1   tablespoon prepared horseradish

Combine salt and pepper; rub over pork. Place in a 13-in. x 9-in. x 2-in. baking pan coated with nonstick cooking spray. Place one sprig of rosemary under the pork and one on top. Bake, uncovered, at 425° for 10 minutes.

Meanwhile, in a saucepan, heat preserves and horseradish until preserves are melted; stir until blended. Remove top rosemary sprig. Brush pork with 1/4 cup pineapple sauce. Bake 10-20 minutes longer or until meat thermometer reads 160°. Let stand for 5 minutes before slicing. Serve with the remaining sauce.

Yield: 4 servings.

Horseradish Help

The brand of horseradish you use will determine the "heat" level in the sauce.

Although horseradish will stay fresh in the refrigerator for up to 3 months, its pungent flavor is best if used within 3 to 4 weeks.

For an early-morning eye opener, stir a bit of horseradish into scrambled eggs or tomato juice.

A dollop of horseradish can also liven up purchased potato salad, coleslaw and French salad dressing.

Broccoli Sausage Simmer

Prep/Total Time: 30 min.

> 1   pound fully cooked kielbasa *or* Polish sausage, cut into 1/4-inch slices
> 1   medium bunch broccoli, cut into florets
> 1/2 cup sliced red onion
> 1   can (14-1/2 ounces) diced tomatoes, undrained
> 1   tablespoon minced fresh basil *or* 1 teaspoon dried basil
> 1   tablespoon minced fresh parsley *or* 1 teaspoon dried parsley flakes
> 1   teaspoon sugar
> 3   cups cooked spiral pasta

In a large skillet, saute sausage, broccoli and onion for 5-6 minutes or until broccoli is crisp-tender. Add the tomatoes, basil, parsley and sugar. Cover and simmer for 10 minutes. Add pasta and heat through.

Yield: 8 servings.

Do-Ahead Ideas

The day before making Broccoli Sausage Supper, slice the sausage and cut up the broccoli and onion. Refrigerate in separate covered containers.

Cook pasta and drain thoroughly. Place in a resealable plastic bag; chill.

Kielbasa Cues

Kielbasa is the generic Polish word for sausage. It comes in dozens of flavors and can be smoked or fresh.

Pork 'n' Veggie Packets

Prep/Total Time: 20 min.

1 **pound pork tenderloin, sliced**
2 **cups broccoli florets**
2 **cups sliced carrots**
1 **can (8 ounces) sliced water chestnuts, drained**
1 **medium green pepper, julienned**
2 **green onions, sliced**
1/4 **cup soy sauce**
4 **teaspoons sesame oil**
1 **teaspoon ground ginger**
Hot cooked rice, optional

Divide pork, broccoli, carrots, water chestnuts, green pepper and onions evenly among four pieces of double-layered heavy-duty foil (about 18 in. x 12 in.). Combine the soy sauce, sesame oil and ginger; drizzle over pork and vegetables. Fold foil around filling and seal tightly.

Grill, covered, over medium heat for 8-10 minutes or until vegetables are tender and pork is no longer pink. Serve with rice if desired.

Yield: 4 servings.

Foiled Again!

Instead of making your own foil packets, pick up a box of heavy-duty foil bags that are sealed on three sides.

Just open the bag, fill with your recipe ingredients and double fold the open end to seal.

After cooking, carefully open to let the steam escape, remove the food and discard the bag.

Bacon-Tomato Bagel Melts

Total Time: 15 min.

2 bagels, split and toasted
8 tomato slices
8 bacon strips, cooked
1 cup (4 ounces) shredded mozzarella cheese
Prepared ranch salad dressing

Place bagel halves cut side up on a baking sheet. Top each with two tomato slices and two bacon strips. Sprinkle with cheese. Broil 5-in. from the heat for 1-2 minutes or until cheese begins to brown. Serve with ranch dressing.

Yield: 4 sandwiches.

Simple Substitutions

You can vary the flavor of Bacon-Tomato Bagel Melts by replacing the regular bacon with Canadian bacon and by using a different flavor of cheese.

If you don't happen to have bagels on hand, toasted English muffins are a tasty substitute.

Pear and Pork Stir-Fry

Prep/Total Time: 20 min.

1/2 cup plum preserves
3 tablespoons soy sauce
2 tablespoons lemon juice
1 tablespoon prepared horseradish
2 teaspoons cornstarch
1/4 teaspoon crushed red pepper flakes
1 medium sweet yellow *or* green pepper, julienned
1/2 to 1 teaspoon minced fresh gingerroot
1 tablespoon vegetable oil
3 medium ripe pears, peeled and sliced
1 pound pork tenderloin, cut into 1/4-inch strips
1 can (8 ounces) sliced water chestnuts, drained
1-1/2 cups fresh *or* frozen snow peas
1 tablespoon sliced almonds, toasted
Hot cooked rice

Pear Pointers

Purchase pears that are fragrant and free of blemishes and soft spots. Pears for eating should be slightly soft at the stem end. Pears to be used in cooking should be somewhat firmer.

Ripen pears at room temperature by placing them in a paper bag. Once ripened, refrigerate pears in a plastic bag for up to 5 days.

In a small bowl, combine the first six ingredients; set aside. In a skillet or wok, stir-fry yellow pepper and ginger in oil for 2 minutes. Add pears; stir-fry for 1 minute or until pepper is crisp-tender. Remove and keep warm.

Stir-fry half of the pork at a time for 1-2 minutes or until meat is no longer pink. Return pear mixture and all of the pork to pan. Add water chestnuts and reserved sauce. Bring to a boil; cook and stir for 2 minutes. Add peas; heat through. Sprinkle with almonds. Serve over rice.

Yield: 4 servings.

Ham Mushroom Fettuccine

Prep/Total Time: 25 min.

12   ounces uncooked fettuccine
3/4   pound fully cooked ham, cubed
2   tablespoons olive oil
1   medium onion, finely chopped
1/2   pound fresh mushrooms, sliced
1   tablespoon all-purpose flour
1/2   teaspoon dried rosemary, crushed
1/4   teaspoon pepper
1-1/4   cups evaporated milk
1/2   cup frozen peas, thawed
2   tablespoons sour cream

Cook fettuccine according to package directions. Meanwhile, in a large skillet, saute ham in oil until lightly browned. Remove with a slotted spoon and set aside.

Add onion to skillet; saute for 4 minutes. Add mushrooms; saute 3 minutes longer. Stir in the flour, rosemary and pepper until blended. Gradually add milk. Bring to a boil; cook and stir for 2 minutes or until thickened. Reduce heat; add peas and sour cream. Cook 2 minutes longer. Drain fettuccine; stir into the mushroom mixture. Add ham; heat through.

Yield: 6 servings.

Lively Leftovers

If you bake a large ham on the weekend, you'll likely have leftovers.

Leftover ham can be refrigerated for 3 to 5 days or frozen for 2 months.

Store a mix of both cubed ham (to use in dishes like Ham Mushroom Fettuccine) and larger pieces (to use in recipes like Glazed Ham Slices on page 179).

Mexicali Pork Chops

Prep/Total Time: 10 min.

1 **envelope taco seasoning**
4 **boneless pork loin chops (1/2 inch thick)**
1 **tablespoon vegetable oil**
Salsa

Rub taco seasoning over pork chops. In a skillet, cook chops in oil over medium-high heat until meat is no longer pink and juices run clear, about 9 minutes. Serve with salsa.

Yield: 4 servings.

Loin Lesson

Loin pork chops are tender, prime chops with a characteristic T-bone on one side.

Leftover cooked pork chops can be refrigerated for up to 4 days or can be frozen for 1 month.

Spicy Seasoning

For folks who like spicy, south-of-the border flavor, look for taco seasoning envelopes marked hot or spicy.

You'll also find reduced-sodium varieties if you're watching your salt intake.

Festive Pork

Prep/Total Time: 20 min.

1	pork tenderloin (3/4 pound), trimmed
1	tablespoon olive oil
1/2	cup beef broth, *divided*
2	tablespoons dried cranberries
1-1/2	teaspoons Dijon mustard
1	tablespoon orange juice concentrate
1	teaspoon cornstarch

Cut tenderloin into 12 slices; flatten to 1/4-in. thickness. Brown in oil in a skillet over medium heat. Add 1/4 cup of beef broth; cover and simmer for 5-10 minutes or until meat is no longer pink. Remove meat to a serving dish and keep warm. Add cranberries, mustard and remaining broth to skillet.

Combine orange juice concentrate and cornstarch until smooth; gradually add to broth mixture, stirring constantly. Bring to a boil; cook and stir for 1-2 minutes. Pour over pork.

Yield: 4 servings.

Substitution Secret

For a richer, full-flavored sauce, use canned beef consomme instead of broth.

Timely Tip

If you don't have a good quality knife at home, ask the butcher to cut the tenderloin into slices and flatten them for you. Then when you get home, you're ready to cook!

Smoked Sausage Skillet

Prep/Total Time: 20 min.

1 **pound fully cooked kielbasa *or* Polish sausage, sliced**
3 **cups shredded cabbage**
1 **celery rib, finely chopped**
1 **tablespoon vegetable oil**
2 **tablespoons Dijon mustard**
1/2 **teaspoon garlic salt**
1/4 **teaspoon rubbed sage**
2 **cups cooked noodles**

In a large skillet, saute the sausage, cabbage and celery in oil for 5 minutes. Add the mustard, garlic salt and sage. Cook and stir over medium heat for 4-6 minutes or until vegetables are tender. Stir in noodles and heat through.

Yield: 4 servings

Cabbage Capers

One large head of cabbage will yield 14 to 16 cups shredded cabbage. Use 4 cups in this recipe, then use leftovers to make Chicken Noodle Stir-Fry (p. 95), Cabbage Turkey Stew (p. 151) and Vegetable Medley (p. 207).

Ham 'n' Broccoli Pizza

Prep/Total Time: 25 min.

1/4 cup process cheese sauce
3 tablespoons prepared ranch salad dressing
1 tablespoon prepared mustard
1/4 teaspoon pepper
1 prebaked Italian bread shell crust
1 cup cubed fully cooked ham
1-1/2 cups broccoli florets
1/2 cup finely chopped onion
3/4 cup shredded Swiss cheese
2 tablespoons grated Parmesan cheese

In a bowl, combine the cheese sauce, salad dressing, mustard and pepper. Place the crust on an ungreased 12-in. pizza pan; spread with cheese mixture. Top with the ham, broccoli and onion. Sprinkle with Swiss and Parmesan cheeses. Bake at 425° for 12-14 minutes or until cheese is melted.

Yield: 4 servings.

Pizza Crust Ideas

Using a prebaked bread shell makes Ham 'n' Broccoli Pizza a snap to prepare.

But feel free to substitute a refrigerated pizza crust, a crust mix or any homemade variety.

Or call your local favorite pizzeria and ask if they sell their own ready-to-bake pizza crusts.

Pork Tenderloin Stir-Fry

Prep/Total Time: 20 min.

1   **pound pork tenderloin,
    thinly sliced**
4   **teaspoons vegetable oil**
8   **fresh mushrooms, sliced**
6   **green onions, sliced**
1/2 **cup frozen peas**
1-1/2 **cups thinly sliced cabbage**
8   **ounces canned bean
    sprouts**
4   **garlic cloves, minced**
2   **teaspoons ground ginger**
1   **teaspoon sugar**
2   **tablespoons soy sauce**
Hot cooked rice

In a skillet, stir-fry pork in oil until no longer pink. Add mushrooms, onions and peas; stir-fry for 1 minute. Add cabbage, bean sprouts, garlic, ginger and sugar; stir-fry for 2 minutes. Stir in soy sauce. Serve over rice.

Yield: 4 servings.

Go Light on the Garlic

Some folks aren't fond of lots of garlic. If your family doesn't care for much of it, use only 2 cloves in this recipe.

Skip the Sprouts

Fresh grated carrots can be substituted for the canned bean sprouts.

Ginger Pork Stir-Fry

Prep/Total Time: 25 min.

1 **tablespoon cornstarch**
1 **cup orange juice**
2 **tablespoons soy sauce**
2 **garlic cloves, minced**
1/4 **teaspoon ground ginger**
1 **pound pork tenderloin,
   cut into thin strips**
1 **tablespoon vegetable oil**
1 **small onion, chopped**
1/4 **pound pea pods *or* snow
   peas**
1/4 **cup chopped sweet red
   pepper**
Hot cooked rice

In a small bowl, combine the cornstarch, orange juice, soy sauce, garlic and ginger until smooth; set aside. In a large skillet or wok, stir-fry pork in oil for 5 minutes or until lightly browned; drain. Add the onion, peas and red pepper; cook and stir for 3-5 minutes or until crisp-tender. Stir orange juice mixture; add to the skillet. Bring to a boil; cook and stir for 2 minutes or until thickened. Serve over rice.

Yield: 4 servings.

Buying Tenderloin

When buying pork tenderloin, look for meat that's firm and grayish pink in color. For the best flavor and tenderness, the meat should have a small amount of marbling.

Look for sales on pork tenderloin and stock up. Use it in 3 to 5 days or freeze for up to 1 year.

Kielbasa Apple Kabobs

Prep/Total Time: 25 min.

1/4 **cup sugar**

1 **tablespoon cornstarch**

3/4 **cup cranberry juice**

2 **tablespoons cider vinegar**

2 **teaspoons soy sauce**

1 **pound fully cooked kielbasa *or* Polish sausage, cut into 1-1/2-inch pieces**

2 **medium tart apples, cut into wedges**

1 **medium sweet red pepper, cut into 1-inch pieces**

1 **medium green pepper, cut into 1-inch pieces**

In a saucepan, combine sugar and cornstarch. Stir in cranberry juice, vinegar and soy sauce. Bring to a boil; cook and stir for 1-2 minutes or until thickened. On metal or soaked wooden skewers, alternately thread sausage, apples and peppers. Grill, uncovered, over indirect medium heat for 8 minutes or until heated through, turning and brushing with glaze occasionally.

Yield: 8 servings.

ABCs of Apples

There are several types of tart apples you can use to make Kielbasa Apple Kabobs, including Baldwin, Cortland, Granny Smith, Jonathan, McIntosh, Northern Spy, Rome Beauty and Winesap.

Select apples that are firm, crisp and deeply colored. Store apples in an open bag in the refrigerator and don't wash until ready to eat or to use in recipes.

Broiled Pork Chops

Prep/Total Time: 20 min.

3/4 cup ketchup
3/4 cup water
2 tablespoons vinegar
1 tablespoon Worcestershire sauce
2 teaspoons brown sugar
1 teaspoon salt
1/2 teaspoon paprika
1/2 teaspoon chili powder
1/8 teaspoon pepper
6 pork loin chops (3/4 inch thick)

In a saucepan, combine the first nine ingredients; bring to a boil. Reduce heat; simmer for 5 minutes, stirring occasionally. Set aside half of the sauce. Place chops on broiling pan rack.

Broil about 4 in. from the heat for 4 minutes on each side. Brush with remaining sauce. Continue broiling, turning and basting occasionally, for 3-4 minutes or until a meat thermometer reads 160°. Serve with reserved sauce.

Yield: 6 servings.

Get Grilling!

When the weather allows, head outside to cook these chops on the grill.

Coat the grill rack with nonstick cooking spray before starting the grill.

Grill, covered, over medium heat for 4-7 minutes on each side or until a meat thermometer reads 160°, basting occasionally.

Stovetop Ham and Penne

Prep/Total Time: 30 min.

12 ounces uncooked penne *or* other medium tube pasta
1/2 cup chopped green onions
5 to 7 garlic cloves, minced
2 tablespoons butter
2 tablespoons olive oil
1 can (28 ounces) diced tomatoes, drained
1-1/2 cups cubed fully cooked ham
1 cup (8 ounces) sour cream
1/2 cup cubed cheddar cheese
1/2 cup cubed Monterey Jack cheese
1/2 cup white wine *or* tomato juice
1 tablespoon minced fresh basil *or* 1 teaspoon dried basil
Salt and pepper to taste

Cook pasta according to package directions. Meanwhile, in a saucepan, saute onions and garlic in butter and oil until tender. Stir in the remaining ingredients; heat through. Drain pasta and place in a bowl; add ham mixture and gently toss to coat.

Yield: 4-6 servings.

Eat Your Veggies

One way to ensure you get enough servings of vegetables in a day is by making a point of serving them as a side dish with your meals.

With your scrambled eggs, toss in fresh sliced mushrooms and sprinkle with chopped tomatoes.

Top lunch sandwiches with leafy green lettuce and tomato slices. Instead of snacking on chips or cookies during the day, reach for baby carrots and celery sticks.

At dinnertime, offer a garden salad or heat up frozen vegetables.

Cran-Orange Pork Tenderloin

Prep/Total Time: 30 min.

1/4   teaspoon garlic salt
1/4   teaspoon pepper
1/8   teaspoon ground mustard
1/8   teaspoon ground cinnamon
  1   pork tenderloin (1 pound)
CRAN-ORANGE SAUCE:
1/2   cup dried cranberries
1/4   cup plus 1 tablespoon
      orange juice, *divided*
1/8   teaspoon ground ginger
Dash ground cloves
  1   can (11 ounces) mandarin
      oranges
  1   tablespoon cornstarch

In a small bowl, combine the first four ingredients; rub over pork. Place on a rack in a shallow roasting pan. Bake, uncovered, at 425° for 25-28 minutes or until a meat thermometer reads 160°.

Meanwhile, in a small saucepan, combine the cranberries, 1/4 cup orange juice, ginger and cloves. Drain oranges, reserving juice; set oranges aside. Add reserved juice to cranberry mixture. Bring to a boil. Reduce heat; cover and simmer for 5 minutes. Combine cornstarch and remaining orange juice until smooth; stir into saucepan. Bring to a boil; cook and stir for 1 minute or until thickened. Fold in oranges. Serve over sliced pork.

Yield: 3-4 servings.

Simple Side

Herbed green beans round out this meaty meal.

In a microwave-safe bowl, combine 1/2 pound fresh green beans, 1 small chopped onion, 2 tablespoons water and 1 clove minced garlic. Cover and microwave on high for 5-7 minutes or until beans are crisp-tender, stirring twice; drain.

Stir in 1/2 teaspoon white wine vinegar and 1/8 teaspoon dried tarragon. Season with salt and pepper to taste.

Smoky Macaroni

Prep/Total Time: 25 min.

1/4 cup chopped sweet red pepper
2 tablespoons chopped onion
1 can (10-3/4 ounces) condensed cheddar cheese soup, undiluted
1 cup milk
1 package (16 ounces) miniature smoked sausages
8 ounces process cheese (Velveeta), cut into 1/2-inch cubes
1 cup frozen peas
4 cups cooked elbow macaroni

In a nonstick skillet, saute red pepper and onion until tender. Combine soup and milk; stir into skillet. Add sausage, cheese and peas. Reduce heat; simmer, uncovered, for 5-10 minutes or until the cheese is melted, stirring occasionally. Add the macaroni; cook 5-10 minutes longer or until heated through.

Yield: 6-8 servings.

Pasta Tip

To get the 4 cups of cooked elbow macaroni needed for this recipe, start with 8 ounces uncooked.

Small Sausages

Miniature smoked sausages are just the right size for the little ones in your family. Plus, you can skip a step of cutting up larger sausages into slices.

Bacon 'n' Egg Sandwiches

Prep/Total Time: 15 min.

1/2   cup sour cream

8   slices bread

4   green onions, chopped

4   slices process American cheese

2   hard-cooked eggs, cut into 1/4-inch slices

8   bacon strips, cooked and drained

1/4   cup butter, softened

Spread sour cream on one side of four slices of bread. Top with onions, cheese, eggs and bacon. Top with the remaining bread. Butter outsides of sandwiches; cook in a large skillet over medium heat until golden brown on both sides.

Yield: 4 servings.

Making Hard-Cooked Eggs

Place eggs in a single layer in a saucepan; add enough cold water to cover by 1 in. Cover and bring to a boil; remove from the heat. Let the eggs stand, covered, in hot water for 15 minutes for large eggs. (Add or subtract 3 minutes for each size larger or smaller.) Rinse in cold water; place eggs in ice water to cool completely.

Hard-cooked eggs can be kept in the refrigerator for a week.

Pork with Orange Sauce

Prep/Total Time: 10 min.

- 1 tablespoon cornstarch
- 1 cup orange juice
- 1 tablespoon jellied cranberry sauce
- 1-1/2 teaspoons soy sauce

Salt and pepper to taste
- 8 slices cooked pork (1/2 inch thick)

In a saucepan, combine cornstarch and orange juice until smooth. Stir in the cranberry sauce, soy sauce, salt and pepper. Bring to a boil; cook and stir for 2 minutes or until thickened. Add pork; heat through.

Yield: 4 servings.

Timeless Taters

Before you begin preparing Pork with Orange Sauce, get some potatoes cooking in the oven.

First, drain two 15-ounce cans of whole white potatoes; place in an ungreased 8-in. square baking dish.

Pour 1/4 cup melted butter over the potatoes. Sprinkle with 1/2 teaspoon seasoned salt, 3 tablespoons grated Parmesan cheese and 1 tablespoon minced fresh parsley. Bake, uncovered, at 350° for 25 minutes.

Savory Sausage and Peppers

Prep/Total Time: 30 min.

1 pound fully cooked kielbasa *or* Polish sausage, cut into 1/2-inch slices

6 tablespoons olive oil

2 medium sweet red peppers, cut into 1-inch chunks

2 medium sweet yellow peppers, cut into 1-inch chunks

2 medium green peppers, cut into 1-inch chunks

2 medium onions, cut into small wedges

2 cups water

2 packages (1.2 ounces *each*) herb and garlic soup mix

1/4 teaspoon hot pepper sauce

Hot cooked rice

In a large skillet, brown sausage in oil over medium-high heat. Remove with a slotted spoon and keep warm. In the drippings, saute peppers and onion until crisp-tender.

In a bowl, combine the water and contents of one soup mix envelope (save the second envelope for another use). Add soup mixture, hot pepper sauce and sausage to the vegetable. Reduce heat; cover and simmer for 5 minutes or until thickened. Serve over rice.

Yield: 4-6 servings.

Pepper Primer

Buy firm, glossy, brightly colored peppers that are unblemished with smooth skins.

Unwashed peppers stay fresh in the refrigerator crisper drawer for up to 1 week.

Wash; remove stems, seeds and membranes before using.

Preparation Pointer

This recipe requires some vegetables to be cut up. Do this the night before (or early in the morning) so you don't have so much to do at dinnertime.

Glazed Ham Slices

Prep/Total Time: 30 min.

2   fully cooked ham slices (about
    1-1/2 pounds and 1/2 inch thick)
2   tablespoons butter
2   cans (8 ounces *each*) sliced
    pineapple
3   teaspoons cornstarch
1/4 cup honey
2   tablespoons steak sauce
2   tablespoons Dijon mustard

Cut ham slice in half. In a skillet, cook ham in butter for 3-4 minutes on each side or until heated through.

Meanwhile, drain pineapple, reserving the juice. Set aside two pineapple slices; refrigerate remaining pineapple for another use. In a bowl, combine cornstarch, pineapple juice, honey, steak sauce and mustard until smooth. Remove ham and keep warm. Add honey mixture to skillet. Bring to a boil over medium-low heat; cook for 1-2 minutes. Return ham to skillet; top with the reserved pineapple slices. Spoon glaze over the top; heat through.

Yield: 4 servings.

Timely Tips

Stop by the deli to have them cut a 1-1/2 pound, 1/2-in.-thick slice of fully cooked ham.

While you're there, pick up an assortment of sides, such as mashed potatoes, green bean casserole or coleslaw.

Sausage and Vegetable Skillet

Prep/Total Time: 25 min.

1/2	pound Italian sausage links, cut into 1/2-inch slices
1	tablespoon vegetable oil
1	cup cubed yellow summer squash
1/2	cup chopped green onions
2	garlic cloves, minced
1-1/2	cups chopped fresh tomatoes
2	teaspoons Worcestershire sauce
1/8	teaspoon cayenne pepper

In a medium skillet, cook sausage in oil over medium heat until no longer pink; drain. Add squash, onions and garlic; cook for 2 minutes. Stir in the tomatoes, Worcestershire sauce and cayenne pepper; heat through.

Yield: 2 servings.

Preparation Pointer

This meal-in-one is terrific for folks cooking for one or two. But it's a breeze to double the recipe for a family of four.

Timely Tip

Instead of chopping the green onions on a cutting board with a knife, mince them with a kitchen scissors.

Spaghetti Pork Chops

Prep: 20 min.   **Cook:** 6 hours

    3 cans (8 ounces *each*) tomato
       sauce
    1 can (10-3/4 ounces) condensed
       tomato soup, undiluted
    1 small onion, finely chopped
    1 bay leaf
    1 teaspoon celery seed
  1/2 teaspoon Italian seasoning
    6 bone-in pork chops
       (1 inch thick)
    2 tablespoons olive oil
Hot cooked spaghetti

In a 5-qt. slow cooker, combine the tomato sauce, soup, onion, bay leaf, celery seed and Italian seasoning. In a large skillet, brown pork chops in oil. Add to the slow cooker. Cover and cook on low for 6-8 hours or until meat is tender. Discard bay leaf. Serve chops and sauce over spaghetti.

Yield: 6 servings.

Bay Leaf Blunder

Be sure to remove the bay leaf before eating a dish that has finished cooking. The whole leaves are used to impart flavor only and are bitter and hard to chew. Plus, they pose a choking hazard.

Simple Sauce

Your favorite variety of spaghetti sauce can be used in place of the tomato sauce, tomato soup, onion and seasonings.

Slow Cooker Cranberry Pork

Prep: 10 min.　**Cook:** 6 hours

- **1** boneless rolled pork loin roast (3 to 4 pounds), halved
- **2** tablespoons vegetable oil
- **1** can (16 ounces) whole-berry cranberry sauce
- **3/4** cup sugar
- **3/4** cup cranberry juice
- **1** teaspoon ground mustard
- **1** teaspoon pepper
- **1/4** teaspoon ground cloves
- **1/4** cup cornstarch
- **1/4** cup cold water

Salt to taste

In a Dutch oven, brown roast in oil on all sides over medium-high heat. Transfer to a 5-qt. slow cooker. Combine the cranberry sauce, sugar, cranberry juice, mustard, pepper and cloves; pour over roast. Cover and cook on low for 6-8 hours or until a meat thermometer reads 160°. Remove roast and keep warm.

In a saucepan, combine cornstarch, water and salt until smooth; stir in cooking juices. Bring to a boil; cook and stir for 2 minutes or until thickened. Serve with roast.

Yield: 9-12 servings.

Easy Entertaining

Don't just serve Slow Cooker Cranberry Roast during the week. It makes an easy yet elegant entree for special occasions as well. While the roast cooks unattended, you can concentrate on side dishes.

Fast Future Meal

Set aside slices of this pork roast and refrigerate. Use to make Pork with Orange Sauce on page 177.

Mandarin Pork Medallions

Prep/Total Time: 30 min.

 1 pork tenderloin (about 1 pound)
 1 tablespoon vegetable oil
3/4 cup orange juice
 1 tablespoon cornstarch
1/4 cup orange marmalade
 2 tablespoons lemon juice
 1 teaspoon prepared horseradish
1/4 to 1/2 teaspoon salt
Hot cooked noodles
 1 can (11 ounces) mandarin oranges, drained

Cut tenderloin into four pieces; pound until 1/3 in. thick. Brown in a large skillet in hot oil for 3 minutes per side; remove and set aside.

Combine orange juice and cornstarch; add to the skillet; cover and cook for 8-10 minutes or until pork is no longer pink. Serve over noodles; garnish with mandarin oranges.

Yield: 4 servings.

Mandarin Orange Facts

The mandarin orange is a small citrus tree with fruit resembling the orange. Varieties include tangerine and clementine. They are less acidic than oranges and are generally sweeter.

Canned mandarin oranges are peeled, sectioned and placed in a light syrup.

Store unopened cans in a cool, dry place for 6 months. Once opened, the fruit should be refrigerated in a covered container and used within 1 week.

Hot Pizza Subs

Prep/Total Time: 25 min.

 1   unsliced loaf (1 pound) Italian bread
 1/4   cup pizza sauce
 1-1/2   teaspoons Italian seasoning
 1   medium green pepper, thinly sliced
 4   slices fully cooked ham
 10   slices salami
 30   slices pepperoni
 4   slices *each* cheddar, mozzarella and American cheese

Slice the bread in half horizontally. Spread the bottom half with pizza sauce; sprinkle with Italian seasoning. Top with green pepper, ham, salami, pepperoni and cheese; replace bread top. Place on a baking sheet. Bake at 425° for 12-15 minutes or until the cheese is melted.

Yield: 4 servings.

Preparation Pointer

Wondering what to do with the remaining can of unused pizza sauce? Serve it alongside Pizza on a Stick (p. 139).

Seasoning Substitution

If you don't have any Italian seasoning on hand, here's an easy substitute.

For 1-1/2 teaspoons seasoning, combine 1/4 each dried oregano leaves, dried marjoram leaves and dried basil leaves and 1/8 teaspoon rubbed sage.

Pork Tenderloin Diane

Prep/Total Time: 20 min.

1 **pork tenderloin (about 1 pound)**
1 **tablespoon lemon-pepper seasoning**
2 **tablespoons butter**
2 **tablespoons lemon juice**
1 **teaspoon Worcestershire sauce**
1 **teaspoon Dijon mustard**
1 **tablespoon minced fresh parsley**

Cut tenderloin into eight pieces; place each piece between two pieces of plastic wrap or waxed paper and flatten to 1/2-in. thickness. Sprinkle with lemon-pepper.

Melt butter in a large skillet over medium heat; cook pork for 3-4 minutes on each side or until no longer pink and juices run clear. Remove to a serving platter and keep warm. To the pan juices, add lemon juice, Worcestershire sauce and mustard; heat through, stirring occasionally. Pour over the pork and sprinkle with parsley. Serve immediately.

Yield: 4 servings.

Simple Sides

Serve Pork Tenderloin Diane with your family's favorite rice mix and these gingered carrots:

Place 4 cups fresh or frozen baby carrots and 2 tablespoons water in a microwave-safe dish. Cover and microwave on high for 9-11 minutes or until tender, stirring twice; drain.

Stir in 2 tablespoons butter, 1/2 teaspoon ground ginger, 1/4 teaspoon salt and 1/8 teaspoon pepper.

Honey-Mustard Pork Scallopini

Prep/Total Time: 20 min.

4   boneless pork chops (about 4 ounces *each*),
      trimmed
2   tablespoons honey
2   tablespoons spicy brown mustard
1/3 cup crushed butter-flavored crackers (about 8
      crackers)
1/3 cup dry bread crumbs
1   tablespoon vegetable oil
1   tablespoon butter

Flatten pork to 1/8-in. thickness. Combine honey and mustard; brush over both sides of pork. In a shallow bowl, combine cracker and bread crumbs; add pork and turn to coat.

In a skillet, heat oil and butter. Fry pork for 2-3 minutes on each side or until crisp and juices run clear.

Yield: 4 servings.

What's in a Name?

Scallopini refers to sauteed cutlets (usually veal or poultry) that have been pounded thin and coated with flour.

This version uses pork and a honey-mustard coating. Try it with veal cutlets sometime, too!

Sausage Bean Stew

Prep/Total Time: 10 min.

- **1** pound fully cooked smoked sausage, halved and cut into 1/4-inch slices
- **2** cans (10 ounces *each*) diced tomatoes and green chilies, undrained
- **1** can (15-1/2 ounces) great northern beans, rinsed and drained
- **1** can (15-1/4 ounces) whole kernel corn, drained
- **1** can (15 ounces) lima beans, drained
- **1** can (15 ounces) black beans, rinsed and drained
- **1/2** teaspoon salt
- **1/8** teaspoon pepper
- **Hot cooked rice, optional**

In a large saucepan, combine the first eight ingredients. Heat through. Serve in bowls over rice if desired.

Yield: 6-8 servings (2 quarts).

Serving Suggestion

This hearty stew can also be served over hot cooked noodles of your choice.

Splendid Substitutions

Sausage Bean Stew is so versatile—you can substitute cubed cooked turkey, chicken, ham or beef for the sausage.

Plus, you can replace the beans with other vegetables of your choice.

Bacon and Pepper Pasta

Prep/Total Time: 30 min.

1/2 pound sliced bacon, diced
  2 medium onions, halved and sliced
  2 garlic cloves, minced
  1 medium green pepper, julienned
  1 medium sweet red pepper, julienned
  1 small jalapeno pepper, seeded and minced
  1 can (14-1/2 ounces) stewed tomatoes
  1 pound linguine *or* pasta of your choice, cooked and drained

In a large skillet, cook bacon until crisp. Remove with a slotted spoon and set aside; reserve drippings. Saute onions and garlic in drippings for 3 minutes. Add peppers; cook and stir for 3 minutes. Stir in tomatoes; heat through. Add bacon and mix well. Serve over pasta.

Editor's Note: When cutting or seeding hot peppers, use rubber or plastic gloves to protect your hands. Avoid touching your face.

Yield: 4 servings.

A Bit About Bacon

Use a kitchen scissors to dice the bacon right into the skillet.

Refrigerate the remaining bacon in a sealed plastic bag and use within 2 weeks.

Seeds Add Spice

To add a little more heat to Bacon and Pepper Pasta, stir in the jalapeno seeds instead of discarding them.

Pork Chops over Rice

Prep/Total Time: 30 min.

8   boneless pork chops (3/4 inch thick)
1   tablespoon vegetable oil
1   cup uncooked long grain rice
1   can (14-1/2 ounces) chicken broth
1/2 cup water
1   small onion, chopped
1   package (10 ounces) frozen peas
1/2 teaspoon salt
1/2 teaspoon dried thyme

In a large skillet over medium heat, brown pork chops in oil; remove. Drain. Add the remaining ingredients to skillet. Place pork chops over the rice mixture. Bring to a boil. Reduce heat; cover and simmer for 20-25 minutes or until rice is tender.

Yield: 8 servings.

Nicer Rice

Replace regular long grain rice with long grain wild rice. Varieties include roasted garlic, vegetable herb and a wild rice and brown rice blend.

Secret Substitution

For added nutrition and color, replace the frozen peas with a 10-ounce bag of frozen mixed vegetables.

Kielbasa and Kidney Beans

Prep/Total Time: 30 min.

1   pound fully cooked kielbasa *or* Polish sausage, cut into 1/2-inch pieces
1   small onion, chopped
1/2 cup chopped sweet red pepper
1/2 cup chopped green pepper
1/4 cup packed brown sugar
2   tablespoons steak sauce
1   tablespoon cider vinegar
1   teaspoon Worcestershire sauce
1   can (15 ounces) white kidney *or* cannellini beans, rinsed and drained

In a skillet, cook sausage for 2-3 minutes. Stir in onion and peppers. Cook and stir until sausage is lightly browned and vegetables are tender; drain. Combine brown sugar, steak sauce, vinegar and Worcestershire sauce; stir into skillet. Add beans. Cook and stir until heated through.

Yield: 4 servings.

Perfect Party Fare

When you have to feed a crowd, consider making several batches of Kielbasa and Kidney Beans. Prepare as directed; transfer to a slow cooker and heat on low during the party.

Set out a variety of fresh breads, butter, fruit salad and purchased cookies for dessert. Then watch the food disappear!

Sweet 'n' Sour Pork Chops

Prep/Total Time: 30 min.

6 boneless pork loin chops
  (1-1/2 pounds)
2 teaspoons vegetable oil
1/2 cup packed brown sugar
1/3 cup balsamic vinegar
1 tablespoon soy sauce
1 teaspoon molasses
1 teaspoon grated orange peel
2 teaspoons cornstarch
1 tablespoon water
2 large navel oranges, peeled
  and sectioned
4 cups hot cooked rice

In a large nonstick skillet, brown pork chops on both sides in oil. Remove and keep warm. In the same pan, combine the brown sugar, vinegar, soy sauce, molasses and orange peel until blended. Return meat to pan; cover and simmer for 15 minutes or until tender. Remove chops and keep warm.

Combine cornstarch and water until smooth; stir into pan juices. Bring to a boil; cook and stir for 2 minutes or until thickened. Add orange segments; cook for 1 minute. Serve over pork and rice.

Yield: 6 servings.

Citrus Secrets

Varieties of oranges include sweet, sour and mandarin (tangerine or Clementine). A navel is a sweet orange.

No matter the variety, buy oranges that feel firm, are brightly colored and are free of bruises.

Oranges stay fresh at room temperature or in the crisper drawer for 2 weeks.

Preparation Pointer

Make a double batch of these saucy pork chops and freeze half for a fast future meal. They reheat nicely so your family will never guess they're eating leftovers.

Ham 'n' Cheese Mashed Potatoes

Prep/Total Time: 30 min.

2 cups mashed potatoes
3/4 teaspoon garlic salt
1 cup diced fully cooked ham
1 cup (4 ounces) shredded cheddar cheese
1/2 cup heavy whipping cream, whipped

In a bowl, combine the potatoes and garlic salt. Spread into a greased 1-1/2-qt. baking dish. Sprinkle with ham. Fold cheese into whipped cream; spoon over ham. Bake, uncovered, at 450° for 15 minutes or until golden brown.

Yield: 4-6 servings.

Classic Casserole

This mashed potato casserole is a new spin on scalloped potatoes and ham. You can make the mashed potatoes from scratch or pick up a pack from your store's refrigerator or freezer section.

Salad on the Side

A green salad topped with assorted fresh vegetables and any kind of salad dressing is all you need to complete this down-home dinner.

Stir-Fried Pork Soup

Prep/Total Time: 30 min.

2/3   pound boneless pork loin,
      cut into thin strips
  1   cup sliced fresh mushrooms
  1   cup chopped celery
1/2   cup diced carrots
  2   tablespoons vegetable oil
  6   cups chicken broth
1/2   cup chopped fresh spinach
  2   tablespoons cornstarch
  3   tablespoons cold water
  1   egg, lightly beaten
Pepper to taste

In a 3-qt. saucepan, stir-fry pork, mushrooms, celery and carrots in oil until pork is browned and vegetables are tender. Add broth and spinach. Combine cornstarch and water to make a thin paste; stir into soup. Return to a boil; boil for 1 minute. Quickly stir in egg. Add pepper. Serve immediately.

Yield: 4-6 servings.

Super Spinach

Spinach is an excellent source of fiber and Vitamins A and C and can be eaten fresh or cooked.

Look for bags of fresh spinach that is already washed and ready to eat.

Fresh spinach should be dried and packed loosely in a cellophane or plastic bag and stored in the refrigerator crisper. If stored properly, it should last 3 or 4 days.

Spicy Sausage Sandwiches

Prep/Total Time: 25 min.

SALSA:
- 2 jalapeno peppers
- 1 large fresh banana pepper
- 1/2 cup diced sweet red pepper
- 1/2 cup diced Vidalia *or* sweet onion
- 1/2 cup frozen corn, thawed
- 1 tablespoon chopped fresh cilantro

SANDWICH:
- 1 pound bulk pork sausage
- 6 English muffins, split and toasted
- 6 slices Colby/Jack cheese

Remove seeds and membranes from jalapeno and banana peppers if desired (for a less spicy salsa). Dice peppers and place in a bowl; add remaining salsa ingredients and mix well. Cover and refrigerate until serving.

Form the sausage into six patties; cook in a skillet over medium heat until meat is no longer pink. Place each on an English muffin half; top with 1 tablespoon salsa and a slice of cheese. Cover with other muffin half. Serve remaining salsa on the side.

Yield: 6 servings.

Speedy Substitute

Instead of forming your own pork sausage patties, pick up a 1-pound package of bratwurst patties from your grocer's meat section.

Time-Saving Tip

You can make the salsa the night before. This not only saves time but allows the flavors to blend.

Tender 'n' Tangy Ribs

Prep: 15 min.   **Cook:** 4 hours

3/4 to 1 cup vinegar
1/2 cup ketchup
   2 tablespoons sugar
   2 tablespoons
      Worcestershire sauce
   1 garlic clove, minced
   1 teaspoon ground mustard
   1 teaspoon paprika
1/2 to 1 teaspoon salt
1/8 teaspoon pepper
   2 pounds pork spareribs
   1 tablespoon vegetable oil

Combine the first nine ingredients in a slow cooker. Cut ribs into serving-size pieces; brown in a skillet in oil. Transfer to slow cooker. Cover and cook on low for 4-6 hours or until tender.

Yield: 2-3 servings.

Buying Ribs

Spareribs are cut from the belly or side of the pig.

Look for meaty ribs with no large areas of fat and with little exposed bone.

Plan on about 1-1/2 servings per pound.

Buy ribs on sale. Refrigerate them for 2 to 3 days. To freeze, wrap well in plastic wrap and freeze for up to 10 months.

Polynesian Sausage Supper

Prep/Total Time: 30 min.

    1   pound fully cooked smoked
        sausage, cut into 1/2-inch slices
    1   medium onion, chopped
    1   medium green pepper, cut into
        1-inch chunks
    1   can (14-1/2 ounces) diced
        tomatoes, undrained
    1/2 cup beef broth
    1   tablespoon brown sugar
    1/4 teaspoon garlic powder
    1/4 teaspoon pepper
    1   can (20 ounces) unsweetened
        pineapple chunks
    2   tablespoons cornstarch
Hot cooked rice

In a large skillet, cook the sausage, onion and green pepper until the meat is no longer pink; drain. Add the tomatoes, broth, brown sugar, garlic powder and pepper. Drain pineapple, reserving juice. Stir pineapple into sausage mixture. Bring to a boil; cook, uncovered, for 5 minutes.

Combine cornstarch and reserved pineapple juice until smooth; gradually add to sausage mixture. Bring to a boil; cook and stir for 2 minutes or until thickened. Serve over rice.

Yield: 6 servings.

Time-Saving Tip

Lots of recipes call for chopped onion. So pick up a pack of frozen chopped onions at your grocery store. It's easy to measure just the amount you needed without the mess of chopping them yourself.

One medium onion is equal to approximately 1/2 cup chopped.

Chunky Spaghetti Sauce

Prep/Total Time: 25 min.

1 **pound bulk Italian sausage**
1 **to 2 medium green peppers, julienned**
1/2 **medium onion, chopped**
1 **garlic clove, minced**
2 **cans (14-1/2 ounces *each*) Italian stewed tomatoes**
1/4 **cup tomato paste**
1-1/2 **teaspoons minced fresh oregano *or* 1/2 teaspoon dried oregano**
1-1/2 **teaspoons minced fresh basil *or* 1/2 teaspoon dried basil**

Hot cooked pasta

Brown sausage in a large saucepan; drain. Add green peppers, onion and garlic; cook until tender, about 5 minutes. Add tomatoes, tomato paste, oregano and basil; simmer, uncovered, for 10-15 minutes. Serve over pasta.

Yield: 4 servings.

Zesty Zucchini

Serve a plate of Chunky Spaghetti Sauce with slices of chilled zucchini.

Slice 2 to 3 medium zucchini; place in a large bowl.

In a small bowl, whisk together 1/3 cup vegetable oil, 1/4 cup white vinegar, 1 teaspoon dried basil, 1/2 teaspoon salt, 1/4 teaspoon pepper and 1/4 teaspoon garlic powder. Pour over zucchini; toss to coat. Chill until serving.

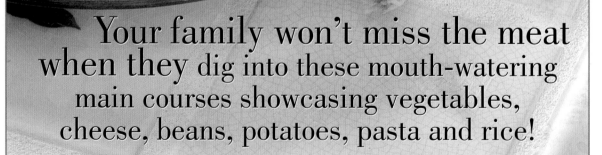

Linguine with Fresh Tomatoes (p. 210)

Your family won't miss the meat
when they dig into these mouth-watering
main courses showcasing vegetables,
cheese, beans, potatoes, pasta and rice!

Make It **Meatless**

Make It Meatless

Mexican Vegetable Pizza (p. 215)

Fresh Veggie Pockets
(p. 213)

Asparagus Cashew Stir-Fry

Prep/Total Time: 20 min.

1 pound fresh asparagus,
  trimmed and cut into 1-inch
  pieces
1/2 cup chopped green onions
1/2 cup chopped sweet red pepper
1 garlic clove, minced
1 teaspoon vegetable oil
2 tablespoons cornstarch
1-1/2 cups vegetable broth
3 tablespoons soy sauce
1/4 teaspoon ground ginger *or*
  3/4 to 1 teaspoon minced
  fresh gingerroot
1/2 cup cashews
1 teaspoon sesame oil
4 cups hot cooked brown rice

In a large nonstick skillet, saute the asparagus, onions, red pepper and garlic in oil until tender. Combine the cornstarch, broth, soy sauce and ginger until blended; add to the skillet. Bring to a boil; cook and stir for 2 minutes or until thickened. Reduce heat; add cashews and sesame oil. Cook 2 minutes longer or until heated through. Serve over rice.

Yield: 4 servings.

Brown Rice Basics

Brown rice contains four times the amount of insoluble fiber found in white rice—a prime reason for eating brown rice instead of white.

To get 4 cups cooked brown rice, start with 1 cup uncooked rice.

Bell Pepper Enchiladas

Prep/Total Time: 30 min.

2 medium green peppers, chopped
1/2 cup shredded cheddar cheese
1/2 cup shredded Monterey Jack cheese
1/2 cup diced process American cheese
4 flour tortillas (8 inches)
1 small jalapeno pepper, minced, optional
1 cup salsa, *divided*
Additional shredded cheese, optional

Sprinkle the green peppers and cheeses down the center of the tortillas; add jalapeno if desired. Roll up. Spread 1/2 cup salsa in a shallow baking dish. Place tortillas seam side down over salsa. Top with remaining salsa. Bake at 350° for 20 minutes or until heated through. Sprinkle with additional cheese if desired.

Editor's Note: When cutting or seeding hot peppers, use rubber or plastic gloves to protect your hands.
Avoid touching your face.

Yield: 4 enchiladas.

Preparation Pointer

Warm tortillas are easier to roll than chilled ones. To heat, wrap tortillas in foil and place in the oven while it's preheating.

Simple Substitutes

For more color, replace one of the green peppers with a red or yellow pepper.

If your family likes a little more spice, use hot pepper Monterey Jack cheese instead of regular Monterey Jack.

The Ultimate Grilled Cheese

Prep/Total Time: 15 min.

  1 package (3 ounces) cream cheese, softened
3/4 cup mayonnaise
  1 cup (4 ounces) shredded cheddar cheese
  1 cup (4 ounces) shredded mozzarella cheese
1/2 teaspoon garlic powder
1/8 teaspoon seasoned salt
 10 slices Italian bread (1/2 inch thick)
  2 tablespoons butter, softened

In a mixing bowl, beat cream cheese and mayonnaise until smooth. Stir in cheeses, garlic powder and seasoned salt. Spread five slices of bread with the cheese mixture, about 1/3 cup on each. Top with remaining bread. Butter the outsides of sandwiches; cook in a large skillet over medium heat until golden brown on both sides.

Yield: 5 servings.

Classic Combo

Who doesn't have fond childhood memories of the classic grilled cheese and tomato soup lunch?

Try this speedy, home-made tomato soup with more grown-up flavor.

Combine 2 cans (28 ounces each) crushed tomatoes and one can (14-1/2 ounces) chicken broth in a large saucepan; bring to a boil. Reduce heat; cover and simmer 10 minutes.

Add 18 minced fresh basil leaves and 1 teaspoon sugar. Reduce heat to low; stir in 1 cup heavy whipping cream and 1/2 cup butter. Cook until butter is melted.

Zippy Zucchini Pasta

Prep/Total Time: 10 min.

1 package (7 ounces) angel hair pasta *or* thin spaghetti
2 small zucchini, sliced 1/4 inch thick
2 garlic cloves, minced
3 tablespoons olive oil
1 can (16 ounces) Mexican diced tomatoes, undrained
1/4 cup minced fresh parsley
1 teaspoon dried oregano
1/8 to 1/2 teaspoon crushed red pepper flakes

Cook pasta according to package directions. Meanwhile, in a skillet, saute zucchini and garlic in oil until zucchini is crisp-tender. Add the tomatoes, parsley, oregano and red pepper flakes; heat through. Drain pasta; top with zucchini mixture.

Yield: 3 servings.

Red Pepper Pointer

A little crushed red pepper flakes goes a long way. Unless you know your family likes spicy foods, start with 1/8 teaspoon in this recipe. Individuals can always sprinkle on more at the table.

Serving Suggestion

While Zippy Zucchini Pasta is a marvelous meatless entree, you can also serve it as a side dish with chicken, pork and turkey.

Three-Cheese Pesto Pizza

Prep/Total Time: 30 min.

1/2 cup chopped red onion
1/2 cup chopped sweet red pepper
1 tablespoon olive oil
1 prebaked Italian bread shell crust (14 ounces)
1/2 cup prepared pesto sauce
1/2 cup chopped ripe olives
1 cup crumbled feta cheese
1 cup (4 ounces) shredded mozzarella cheese
1 cup shredded Parmesan cheese
2 plum tomatoes, thinly sliced

In a skillet, saute onion and red pepper in oil until tender. Place crust on an ungreased 12-in. pizza pan; spread with pesto. Top with onion mixture, olives, cheeses and tomatoes. Bake at 400° for 15-20 minutes or until cheese is melted.

Yield: 4 servings.

Homemade Pesto

When fresh basil is in full bloom in your garden, make 3/4 cup of homemade pesto!

In a food processor or blender, place 1 cup tightly packed fresh basil leaves, 1 cup tightly packed fresh parsley leaves, 1 to 2 minced garlic cloves, 1/2 cup olive oil, 1/2 cup grated Parmesan cheese and 1/4 teaspoon salt.

Cover and process on high until pureed. Freeze 1/4-cup portions in tightly covered containers for up to 6 months.

Make It **Meatless**

Tomato Spinach Spirals

Prep/Total Time: 25 min.

- 1 package (8 ounces) spiral pasta
- 1 package (10 ounces) frozen creamed spinach
- 1 can (15 ounces) diced tomatoes, undrained
- 3 tablespoons grated Romano cheese, *divided*
- 3 tablespoons grated Parmesan cheese, *divided*
- 1/2 teaspoon salt

Cook pasta according to package directions. Meanwhile, prepare spinach according to package directions. Drain pasta; place in a bowl. Add the spinach, tomatoes, 2 tablespoons of Romano cheese, 2 tablespoons of Parmesan cheese and salt; toss. Sprinkle with the remaining cheese.

Yield: 6 servings.

Cooking Pasta

When cooking pasta, use a pot large enough for the pasta to move around. Pasta expands while cooking, so if there isn't enough water, the pasta will become gummy.

Add pasta to the pan when the water comes to a full, rolling boil.

Pasta should only be cooked until "al dente" or when it gives a little when you bite into it and it's tender but not mushy.

Pasta Primavera

Prep/Total Time: 25 min.

1 cup sliced onion

1 cup julienned green *or* sweet red pepper

4 teaspoons olive oil

1 cup sliced zucchini

1 cup sliced yellow summer squash

4 medium fresh mushrooms, sliced

1-1/2 cups stewed tomatoes

1/2 to 1 teaspoon dried basil

4 cups hot cooked pasta

Shredded Parmesan cheese, optional

In a skillet, saute onion and green pepper in oil until crisp-tender. Add zucchini, yellow squash and mushrooms; saute for 1 minute. Add tomatoes and basil. Bring to a boil; reduce heat. Cover and simmer for 8-10 minutes or until vegetables are tender. Toss with pasta; sprinkle with cheese if desired.

Yield: 4 servings.

Primavera Lesson

Primavera is Italian for "spring style," which refers to the use of fresh vegetables as a seasoning or garnish in a dish.

Stewed Tomato Secret

Bits of onions, celery and green pepper flavor stewed tomatoes so you don't want to drain them before adding to dishes. Try using Italian-style stewed tomatoes in this recipe.

Vegetable Medley

Prep/Total Time: 25 min.

- 1 teaspoon chicken bouillon granules
- 1/4 cup water
- 1 teaspoon salt
- 1/4 teaspoon garlic powder
- 1/4 teaspoon pepper
- 1 teaspoon plus 1 tablespoon olive oil, *divided*
- 2 cups broccoli florets
- 2 medium carrots, thinly sliced
- 1 large onion, sliced and quartered
- 1 cup sliced celery
- 2 medium zucchini, halved lengthwise and thinly sliced
- 1 medium sweet red pepper, thinly sliced
- 1 cup sliced fresh mushrooms
- 2 cups thinly sliced cabbage

In a small saucepan, heat bouillon and water for 1 minute; stir well. Stir in the salt, garlic powder, pepper and 1 teaspoon oil.

In a large nonstick skillet or wok, stir-fry the broccoli, carrots, onion and celery in remaining oil for 2-3 minutes. Add the bouillon mixture; cook and stir for 3 minutes. Add zucchini and red pepper; stir-fry for 3 minutes. Add mushrooms and cabbage; stir-fry 1-2 minutes longer or until crisp-tender. Serve immediately.

Yield: 8 servings.

Hot Stir-Frying Tips

Remember that smaller vegetable pieces cook faster than larger ones.

Start stir-frying more dense vegetables first. For instance, carrot coins take longer to cook than sliced peppers or mushrooms.

Serving Suggestion

Cook some rice to serve with this veggie stir-fry. In general, plan on 1/2 cup of rice per person.

Citrus Veggie Stir-Fry

Prep: 10 min.   **Cook:** 15 min.

- 1 tablespoon cornstarch
- 1 cup orange juice
- 2 tablespoons balsamic vinegar
- 2 garlic cloves, minced
- 1 teaspoon grated orange peel
- 1/2 teaspoon ground ginger
- 1/8 teaspoon hot pepper sauce
- 1 cup sliced carrots
- 1 cup julienned sweet red pepper
- 1 cup julienned green pepper
- 1 tablespoon vegetable oil
- 1 cup sliced fresh mushrooms
- 2 cups fresh *or* frozen snow peas
- 1/2 cup sliced green onions
- 1/3 cup salted cashews
- 4 cups hot cooked rice

Preparation Pointer

Before peeling an orange, use a citrus zester to remove the peel. Freeze the zest in a small heavy-duty resealable plastic bag for up 6 months to use in a variety of recipes.

Serving Suggestion

Put the hot pepper sauce on the table for family members who want to add a little more spice.

In a bowl, combine the first seven ingredients until blended; set aside. In a large nonstick skillet or wok, stir-fry carrots and peppers in oil for 5 minutes. Add mushrooms and snow peas; stir-fry for 6 minutes. Add green onions; stir-fry for 3 minutes or until the vegetables are crisp-tender.

Stir orange juice mixture and add to pan. Bring to a boil; cook and stir for 2 minutes or until thickened. Stir in cashews. Serve with rice.

Yield: 4 servings.

Veggie Burgers

Prep/Total Time: 15 min.

1 small zucchini, grated
1 medium uncooked potato,
   peeled and grated
1 medium carrot, grated
1/4 cup grated onion
3/4 cup egg substitute
Pepper to taste
12 slices whole wheat bread, toasted
Sliced red onion and lettuce leaves,
   optional

In a bowl, combine the first six ingredients; mix well. Pour about 1/2 cup batter onto a hot griddle lightly coated with nonstick cooking spray. Fry for 2-3 minutes on each side or until golden brown. Serve on toasted bread with onion and lettuce if desired.

Yield: 6 burgers.

Want Fries with That?

Baked Basil Fries have a pleasant taste that pairs well with these burgers.

Cut four medium red potatoes into 1/4-in. sticks. In a bowl, combine 1/4 cup grated Parmesan cheese, 1 tablespoon olive oil, 1 tablespoon fresh basil and 1/4 teaspoon garlic powder. Add potato sticks; toss to coat.

Place in a greased 15-in. x 10-in. baking pan. Bake at 425° for 15 minutes; turn potatoes. Bake 15-20 minutes more or until crisp and tender.

Linguine with Fresh Tomatoes

Prep/Total Time: 15 min.

8 ounces uncooked linguine
3 medium tomatoes, chopped
6 green onions, sliced
1/2 cup grated Parmesan cheese
1/4 cup minced fresh basil *or* 4
    teaspoons dried basil
2 garlic cloves, minced
1 teaspoon salt
1/2 teaspoon pepper
3 tablespoons butter

Cook pasta according to package directions. Meanwhile, in a large serving bowl, combine the tomatoes, onions, Parmesan cheese, basil, garlic, salt and pepper. Drain pasta and toss with butter. Add to the tomato mixture; toss to coat.

Yield: 6 servings.

Tomato Tip

Buy tomatoes that are firm, well-shaped and fragrant. They should be free from blemishes.

Store tomatoes at room temperature away from direct sunlight and use within a few days. Don't refrigerate tomatoes...it will make the flesh pulpy and destroy the flavor.

Beefsteak tomatoes are terrific for this recipe because they're flavorful but are less juicy than other varieties.

Pepper-Topped Pizza

Prep/Total Time: 30 min.

- 1 tube (12 ounces) refrigerated flaky buttermilk biscuits
- 1 tablespoon olive oil
- 1/2 cup chopped green pepper
- 1/2 cup chopped sweet yellow pepper
- 1/2 cup chopped tomato
- 1/4 cup chopped onion
- 1/2 teaspoon garlic powder
- 1/4 teaspoon dried basil
- 1/4 teaspoon dried oregano
- 1/4 cup shredded Parmesan cheese

Preparation Pointers

A refrigerated pizza crust can be used in place of the biscuits. Spread it out onto a 12-in. pizza pan or in a 13-in. x 9-in. baking pan. Add the pizza toppings and bake according to the package directions.

If your family favors saucy suppers, skip the oil and spread pizza sauce on the crust before topping with vegetables.

Split biscuits in half horizontally. Arrange on a lightly greased 12-in. round pizza pan; press dough together to seal the edges. Brush with oil. Sprinkle with peppers, tomato, onion, garlic powder, basil and oregano.

Bake at 400° for 15-20 minutes or until crust is golden brown. Cover edges with foil to prevent overbrowning if necessary. Sprinkle with Parmesan cheese. Serve immediately.

Yield: 4-6 servings.

Egg and Broccoli Casserole

Prep: 10 min. **Cook:** 3-1/2 hours

1 carton (24 ounces) small-curd cottage cheese

1 package (10 ounces) frozen chopped broccoli, thawed and drained

2 cups (8 ounces) shredded cheddar cheese

6 eggs, beaten

1/3 cup all-purpose flour

1/4 cup butter, melted

3 tablespoons finely chopped onion

1/2 teaspoon salt

Additional shredded cheddar cheese, optional

In a large bowl, combine the first eight ingredients. Pour into a greased slow cooker. Cover and cook on high for 1 hour. Stir. Reduce heat to low; cover and cook 2-1/2 to 3 hours longer or until a thermometer placed in the center reads 160° and the eggs are set. Sprinkle with cheese if desired.

Yield: 6 servings.

Sunny-Side Supper

This no-fuss egg casserole cooks for a few hours, making it perfect for dinner on days when you have an afternoon at home.

Store-bought muffins and fruit salad easily round out the meal. For meat lovers, serve cooked bacon or Canadian bacon the side.

Fresh Veggie Pockets

Prep/Total Time: 15 min.

> 1 carton (8 ounces) spreadable cream cheese
> 1/4 cup sunflower kernels
> 1 teaspoon seasoned salt
> 4 wheat pita breads, halved
> 1 medium tomato, thinly sliced
> 1 medium cucumber, thinly sliced
> 1 cup sliced fresh mushrooms
> 1 ripe avocado, peeled and sliced

In a bowl, combine the cream cheese, sunflower kernels and seasoned salt; spread about 2 tablespoons on the inside of each pita half. Layer with tomato, cucumber, mushrooms and avocado.

Yield: 4 servings.

Pick Up Pitas

Skip ordinary bread and prepare vegetable sandwiches with pita! Pita bread is a flat round bread made from white or whole wheat flour that is traditional in many Middle Eastern and Mediterranean cuisines.

Serving Suggestion

Use any ingredients you'd like in the Fresh Veggie Pockets. Other ideas include fresh spinach leaves, julienned bell pepper, thinly sliced zucchini and alfalfa sprouts.

Black Bean Rice Burgers

Prep/Total Time: 20 min.

1 can (15 ounces) black beans, rinsed and drained
1 cup cooked brown rice
1 small onion, finely chopped
1 egg, lightly beaten
2 tablespoons plus 1/4 cup salsa, *divided*
1/4 cup sour cream
4 lettuce leaves
4 slices cheddar cheese (1 ounce *each*)
4 hamburger buns, split

In a large bowl, mash beans with a fork. Add the rice, onion, egg and 2 tablespoons salsa; mix well. Drop by 1/2 cupfuls into a large nonstick skillet coated with nonstick cooking spray. Flatten to 1/2-in. thickness. Cook over medium heat for 4-5 minutes on each side or until firm and browned.

In a small bowl, combine the sour cream and remaining salsa. Place a lettuce leaf, burger, sour cream mixture and slice of cheese on the bun.

Yield: 4 servings.

Black Bean Basics

Black beans have long been a protein staple in cultures all over the world. The slightly sweet flavor and creamy texture appeals to many palates.

Canned black beans can be a real timesaver for busy cooks. Unopened cans stay fresh in the pantry for up to 1 year. Drain and rinse thoroughly before using.

Mexican Vegetable Pizza

Prep/Total Time: 30 min.

1/2 small onion, chopped
1 teaspoon chili powder
1/2 teaspoon ground cumin
1/4 teaspoon ground cinnamon
1 tablespoon water
1 can (15 ounces) black beans, rinsed and drained
1/4 cup canned diced green chilies
1 package (16 ounces) prebaked Italian bread shell crust
1 cup salsa
1 cup (4 ounces) shredded cheddar cheese, *divided*
3/4 cup chopped fresh tomato
1/2 cup frozen corn, thawed
1/2 cup chopped green pepper
3 tablespoons sliced ripe olives, drained
1/2 cup sour cream

In a nonstick skillet coated with nonstick cooking spray, combine the onion, chili powder, cumin, cinnamon and water. Cover and cook for 3-4 minutes. Remove from the heat; stir in beans and chilies. Transfer half of the bean mixture to a food processor; cover and process until almost smooth.

Spread pureed bean mixture over the crust. Spread with salsa. Top with half of the cheese and remaining bean mixture. Sprinkle with tomato, corn, green pepper, olives and remaining cheese. Bake at 450° for 10-12 minutes or until crust is golden brown. Serve with sour cream.

Yield: 8 servings.

Serving Suggestion

This zesty pizza can also be served as an appetizer at your next gathering with friends. Just cut it into smaller squares instead of into slices.

Speedy Substitution

When you're really pressed for time, you can skip the first part of the recipe by reaching for a can of re-fried beans. Remove from the can; mash and spread over the crust.

10-Minute Taco Salad

Prep/Total Time: 10 min.

2 cans (16 ounces *each*) chili beans, undrained
1 package (10-1/2 ounces) corn chips
2 cups (8 ounces) shredded cheddar cheese
4 cups chopped lettuce
2 small tomatoes, chopped
1 small onion, chopped
1 can (2-1/4 ounces) sliced ripe olives, drained
1-1/4 cups salsa
1/2 cup sour cream

In a saucepan or microwave-safe bowl, heat the beans. Place corn chips on a large platter. Top with beans, cheese, lettuce, tomatoes, onion, olives, salsa and sour cream. Serve immediately.

Yield: 8 servings.

Preparation Pointers

Present this salad in purchased tortilla salad bowls instead of over corn chips.

Or serve it as a snack by replacing the corn chips with tortilla chips and cutting back on the lettuce.

Where's the Beef?

Make this a meaty main-dish salad by adding some taco-seasoned ground beef.

Microwave Mac 'n' Cheese

Prep/Total Time: 30 min.

2 cups uncooked elbow macaroni
2 cups hot water
1/3 cup butter
1/4 cup chopped onion
3/4 teaspoon salt
1/4 teaspoon pepper
1/4 teaspoon ground mustard
1/3 cup all-purpose flour
1-1/4 cups milk
8 ounces process cheese (Velveeta), cubed

In a 2-qt. microwave-safe dish, combine the first seven ingredients. Cover and microwave on high for 3-1/2 minutes; stir. Cover and cook at 50% powder for 4 minutes or until mixture comes to a boil, rotating a half turn once.

Combine flour and milk until smooth; stir into macaroni mixture. Add cheese. Cover and cook on high for 6-8 minutes or until the macaroni is tender and sauce is bubbly, rotating a half turn once and stirring every 3 minutes.

Editor's Note: This recipe was tested in an 850-watt microwave.

Yield: 4 servings.

Mexican Macaroni

Turn this macaroni and cheese dinner into Southwestern fare by using Mexican process cheese. It contains jalapeno peppers and comes in mild and hot flavors.

Serving Suggestion

Macaroni and cheese is a hearty meal in itself. But it can also be served as a side dish alongside any meaty entree.

Italian Bow Tie Bake

Prep/Total Time: 30 min.

  8 ounces uncooked bow tie pasta
  1 jar (16 ounces) garlic and onion spaghetti sauce
  1 envelope Italian salad dressing mix
  2 cups (8 ounces) shredded mozzarella cheese

Cook pasta according to package directions; drain. In a bowl, combine the spaghetti sauce and salad dressing mix; add pasta and toss to coat. Transfer to a greased shallow 2-qt. baking dish. Sprinkle with cheese. Bake, uncovered, at 400° for 15-20 minutes or until heated through.

Yield: 4 servings.

Preparation Pointers

For a more mellow flavor, eliminate the Italian salad dressing mix.

And feel free to experiment with any variety of spaghetti sauce you like.

Meaty Variation

For an even heartier casserole, combine the spaghetti sauce with 1 pound cooked ground beef or turkey.

Greek Hero

Prep/Total Time: 15 min.

2 tablespoons lemon juice
1 tablespoon olive oil
1 can (15 ounces) garbanzo beans *or* chickpeas, rinsed and drained
2 garlic cloves, minced
1 teaspoon dried oregano
1/4 teaspoon salt
1/8 teaspoon pepper

SANDWICH:
1 unsliced loaf (8 ounces) French bread
2 medium sweet red peppers, cut into thin strips
1/2 medium cucumber, sliced
2 small tomatoes, sliced
1/4 cup thinly sliced red onion
1/4 cup chopped ripe olives
1/4 cup chopped stuffed olives
1/2 cup crumbled feta cheese
4 lettuce leaves

For hummus, place the lemon juice, oil and beans in a food processor; cover and process until smooth. Add garlic, oregano, salt and pepper; mix well.

Slice bread in half horizontally. Carefully hollow out bottom half, leaving a 1/2-in shell. Spread hummus into shell. Layer with the red peppers, cucumber, tomatoes, onion, olives, cheese and lettuce. Replace bread top. Cut into four portions.

Yield: 4 servings.

Hummus Hint

Hummus is a protein-rich Middle Eastern dish typically made from chickpeas, lemon juice, garlic and olive or sesame oil. It is popular as a dip and spread.

Instead of making the hummus from scratch, you can pick up some prepared hummus at most grocery stores.

Cast aside everyday
dinners and net
some compliments with
an assortment of
from-the-sea favorites!

Nut-Crusted
Fried Fish (p. 239)

Fast **Fish & Seafood**

Fast Fish & Seafood

Garlic Shrimp Stir-Fry (p. 225)

Seasoned Fish Sticks

Prep/Total Time: 30 min.

  1 teaspoon paprika
  1 teaspoon chili powder
  1/2 teaspoon garlic powder
  1/2 teaspoon onion powder
  1/2 teaspoon ground cumin
  1/4 teaspoon cayenne pepper
  2 tablespoons vegetable oil, *divided*
  2 packages (8 ounces *each*) frozen breaded fish sticks

In a small bowl, combine the first six ingredients; mix well. Transfer half of the seasoning mix to a large resealable plastic bag; set aside. Place 1 tablespoon oil in a large resealable plastic bag; add half of fish sticks and shake to coat. Transfer fish to resealable bag with seasonings and shake to coat.

Place in a single layer in an ungreased baking sheet. Repeat with remaining ingredients. Bake at 400° for 18-22 minutes or until golden brown.

Yield: 4 servings.

Mmm... Mac 'n' Cheese!

Fish sticks and macaroni and cheese is a supper that will appeal to kids of all ages!

In a medium saucepan, bring 6 cups water to a boil. Add one package (7-1/4 ounces) macaroni and cheese dinner mix; set aside cheese packet. Cook according to package directions. Drain and return to saucepan.

Add one can (10 ounces) diced tomatoes and green chilies and 1/4 cup butter; mix until butter is melted.

Add the reserved cheese packet and mix well. Remove from the heat; add 1/2 cup grated Parmesan and 1/2 cup shredded mozzarella cheese.

Sunshine Halibut

Prep/Total Time: 30 min.

1/3 cup chopped onion

1 garlic clove, minced

2 tablespoons minced fresh parsley

1/2 teaspoon grated orange peel

4 halibut steaks (4 ounces *each*)

1/4 cup orange juice

1 tablespoon lemon juice

1/4 teaspoon salt

1/4 teaspoon lemon-pepper seasoning

In a nonstick skillet coated with nonstick cooking spray, saute onion and garlic until tender; remove from the heat. Stir in parsley and orange peel.

Place halibut in an 8-in. square baking dish coated with nonstick cooking spray. Top with onion mixture. Combine orange and lemon juices; pour over fish. Sprinkle with salt and lemon-pepper. Cover and bake at 400° for 15-20 minutes or until fish flakes easily with a fork.

Yield: 4 servings.

Testing Fish for Doneness

You can't test fish for doneness with a thermometer. Instead, gently insert the tines of a fork into the thickest part of the fish and wiggle the fork slightly.

When the fish is done, it will flake easily. The flesh will look evenly white and opaque with no more translucent quality.

Cucumber Tuna Boats

Prep/Total Time: 15 min.

3 medium cucumbers, seeded
1 can (6 ounces) tuna, drained and flaked
2 hard-cooked eggs, chopped
1/2 cup shredded cheddar cheese
1/2 cup diced celery
1/4 cup mayonnaise
2 tablespoons sweet pickle relish
1 tablespoon finely chopped onion
1 teaspoon lemon juice
1/2 teaspoon salt

Cut a thin slice from bottom of each cucumber if necessary so it sits flat. In a bowl, combine the remaining ingredients. Spoon into the cucumbers.

Yield: 3 servings.

Seeding a Cuke

Cut the cucumber in half lengthwise. With a teaspoon, scrape out the seeds and discard.

Which Spread to Use

Mayonnaise and salad dressing are interchangeable in most recipes.

Mayonnaise is a thick, creamy sauce made with oil, egg yolks, lemon juice or vinegar and seasonings.

Salad dressing doesn't contain egg yolks and is generally sweeter than mayonnaise.

Garlic Shrimp Stir-Fry

Prep/Total Time: 15 min.

- 4 garlic cloves, minced
- 2 tablespoons butter
- 1 pound uncooked medium shrimp, peeled and deveined
- 6 ounces fresh snow peas
- 1/2 cup julienned sweet red pepper
- 1/2 cup julienned sweet yellow pepper
- 3 tablespoons minced fresh basil *or* 1 tablespoon dried basil
- 3 tablespoons minced fresh parsley
- 1/2 teaspoon salt
- 1/4 teaspoon pepper
- 1/4 cup chicken broth

Hot cooked rice

In a large skillet, saute garlic in butter until tender. Add the shrimp, peas, peppers, basil, parsley, salt and pepper. Stir-fry for 5 minutes or until shrimp turn pink and vegetables are crisp-tender. Add broth. Cook 1 minute longer or until heated through. Serve over rice.

Yield: 4 servings.

Peeling and Deveining Shrimp

Remove the shell from the raw shrimp by opening the shell at the underside of the leg area and peeling it back.

To remove the black vein, make a slit with a paring knife along the back from the head to the tail. Rinse under cold water to remove the exposed vein.

Confetti Salmon Steaks

Prep/Total Time: 10 min.

 2 salmon steaks (6 ounces *each*)
 1/2 teaspoon Worcestershire sauce
 1/2 teaspoon lemon juice
 1/2 teaspoon Cajun *or* Creole seasoning
 1/4 teaspoon salt
 1/2 cup diced green pepper
 1/2 cup diced sweet red pepper

Place the salmon in an ungreased 8-in. square microwave-safe dish. Rub with Worcestershire sauce and lemon juice; sprinkle with Cajun seasoning and salt. Sprinkle peppers on top.

Cover and microwave on high for 5-1/2 to 6 minutes, turning once, or until fish flakes easily with a fork. Let stand, covered, for 2 minutes.

Editor's Note: This recipe was tested in an 850-watt microwave.

Yield: 2 servings.

Salmon Facts

Salmon is an excellent source of omega-3 fatty acids and is considered to be a "super food."

When buying fresh salmon, it should have a deep, "salmon pink" color. The meat should have a slight sheen, appear somewhat translucent and have smooth cuts. Cuts of salmon that have gaps are indicative of old fish.

Use fresh salmon within 2 days of purchase. It can be frozen for 2 to 3 months.

Grilled Fish Sandwiches

Prep/Total Time: 30 min.

    4   cod fillets (4 ounces *each*)
    1   tablespoon lime juice
1/2   teaspoon lemon-pepper seasoning
1/4   cup mayonnaise
    2   teaspoons Dijon mustard
    1   teaspoon honey
    4   hamburger buns, split
    4   lettuce leaves
    4   tomato slices

Brush both sides of fillets with lime juice; sprinkle with lemon-pepper. Coat grill rack with nonstick cooking spray before starting the grill. Grill fillets, covered, over medium heat for 5-6 minutes on each side or until fish flakes easily with a fork.

In a small bowl, combine the mayonnaise, mustard and honey. Spread over the bottom of each bun. Top with a fillet, lettuce and tomato; replace bun tops.

Yield: 4 servings.

Soup on the Side

A good-quality canned soup turns these fish sandwiches into a complete meal.

Timely Tip

Replace the cod fillets and seasonings with frozen grilled fish fillets. They come in a variety of flavors (like lemon-pepper, garlic butter and Cajun) and cook in a matter of minutes.

Seared Salmon with Balsamic Sauce

Prep/Total Time: 30 min.

4 salmon fillets (4 ounces *each*)
1/2 teaspoon salt
1/4 teaspoon pepper
2 teaspoons vegetable oil
1/4 cup water
1/4 cup balsamic vinegar
4-1/2 teaspoons lemon juice
4 teaspoons brown sugar

Sprinkle both sides of fillets with salt and pepper. In a large nonstick skillet, cook salmon in oil over medium heat for 10-15 minutes or until fish flakes easily with a fork, turning once. Remove and keep warm.

Combine the water, vinegar, lemon juice and brown sugar; pour into skillet. Bring to a boil; cook until liquid is reduced to about 1/3 cup. Serve over salmon.

Yield: 4 servings.

Balsamic Basics

True balsamic vinegar is made from the unfermented juice of white grapes known as "must." The best varieties have nothing else added to them—only the grapes.

True balsamic is very dark in color and has a sweet, fruity flavor and syrup-like consistency.

Bottles of balsamic vinegar come in a variety of sizes and price ranges. Read the ingredients and purchase a bottle that suits your budget.

Shrimp Fried Rice

Prep/Total Time: 20 min.

- 4 tablespoons butter, *divided*
- 4 eggs, lightly beaten
- 3 cups cold cooked rice
- 1 package (16 ounces) frozen mixed vegetables
- 1 pound uncooked medium shrimp, peeled and deveined
- 1/2 teaspoon salt
- 1/4 teaspoon pepper
- 8 bacon strips, cooked and crumbled, optional

In a large skillet, melt 1 tablespoon butter over medium-high heat. Pour eggs into skillet. As eggs set, lift edges, letting uncooked portion flow underneath. Remove eggs and keep warm.

Melt remaining butter in the skillet. Add rice, vegetables and shrimp; cook and stir for 5 minutes or until shrimp turn pink. Return eggs to the pan; sprinkle with salt and pepper. Cook until heated through. Sprinkle with bacon if desired.

Yield: 8 servings.

Timely Tips

Why order takeout Chinese food when you can make your own at home? Shrimp Fried Rice has plenty of make-ahead qualities that make it perfect for weekday dining.

Start by scrambling the eggs; let cool and place in an airtight container. Refrigerate.

Cook about 1-1/2 cups instant rice to yield 3 cups. Cool, cover and chill.

Speedy Salmon Patties

Prep/Total Time: 20 min.

  2   cans (12 ounces *each*) boneless skinless salmon, drained
2/3   cup finely chopped onion
  2   eggs
 10   saltines, crushed
  1   teaspoon Worcestershire sauce
1/2   teaspoon salt
1/4   teaspoon pepper
  4   teaspoons butter

In a bowl, combine the first seven ingredients; mix well. Shape into six patties. In a skillet, fry patties in butter over medium heat for 3-4 minutes on each side or until heated through.

Yield: 6 servings.

Preparation Pointer

Salmon sold in 12-ounce cans has already been boned and skinned, saving you the task of doing that at home.

If your store doesn't carry this kind of canned salmon, use two 14-1/2-ounce cans; remove bones and skin after draining.

Canned salmon can be stored in the pantry for up to a year. So it's great to have on hand for meals in minutes.

Scallops with Spaghetti

Prep/Total Time: 25 min.

- 1 package (7 ounces) spaghetti
- 1 pound sea scallops
- 4 garlic cloves, minced
- 2 tablespoons olive oil
- 1 tablespoon butter
- 1-1/2 cups julienned carrots
- 1-1/2 cups frozen French-style green beans, thawed
- 1 sweet red pepper, julienned
- 2 tablespoons lemon juice
- 1 tablespoon minced fresh parsley
- 1 tablespoon minced fresh basil *or* 1 teaspoon dried basil
- 1/4 teaspoon salt
- 1/8 teaspoon pepper

Cook spaghetti according to package directions. Meanwhile, in a large skillet or wok, stir-fry scallops and garlic in oil and butter for 5 minutes or until scallops are opaque; remove and keep warm.

In the same skillet, stir-fry the carrots, beans and red pepper until crisp-tender. Stir in the lemon juice, parsley, basil, salt and pepper. Drain spaghetti. Add scallops and spaghetti to the vegetable mixture; toss to coat.

Yield: 4 servings.

Scallop Lesson

Sea scallops can range from 1/2 to 1 inch thick. To cook thicker scallops more quickly, cut them in half horizontally.

Overcooking scallops makes them tough and rubbery. It's best to cook them quickly by sauteing, grilling, broiling or poaching.

Grilled Sole with Nectarines

Prep/Total Time: 15 min.

- 4 sole fillets (6 ounces *each*)
- 2 medium nectarines *or* peaches, peeled and sliced
- 1/2 cup sliced green onions
- 1-1/2 teaspoons chopped fresh tarragon *or* 1/2 teaspoon dried tarragon
- 1/4 teaspoon salt
- 1/8 teaspoon pepper
- 1 teaspoon butter, melted

Place each fillet on a double thickness of heavy-duty foil (about 18 in. x 12 in.). Arrange nectarines around the fillets. Sprinkle with green onions, tarragon, salt, pepper and butter. Fold foil around fish and seal tightly. Grill, covered, over medium heat for 7-8 minutes or until fish flakes easily with a fork.

Yield: 4 servings.

Nectarine Know-How

Look for fragrant, brightly colored nectarines that give slightly to palm pressure. Avoid any with bruises or that are hard.

Store ripe nectarines in the refrigerator for up to 5 days.

Save some time and skip the step of peeling the nectarines before putting on top of the fish.

Substitution Secret

Tilapia, perch or flounder can be used in place of sole.

232

Deviled Crab Casserole

Prep/Total Time: 30 min.

2	cans (6 ounces *each*) crabmeat, drained, flaked and cartilage removed
2	cups dry bread crumbs, *divided*
1-1/2	cups milk
1/2	cup chopped green onions
4	hard-cooked eggs, chopped
1	teaspoon salt
1/2	teaspoon Worcestershire sauce
1/4	teaspoon ground mustard
1/4	teaspoon pepper
3/4	cup butter, melted, *divided*

Paprika

In a bowl, combine crab, 1-1/2 cups bread crumbs, milk, onions, eggs, salt, Worcestershire sauce, mustard and pepper. Add 1/2 cup butter; mix well. Spoon into a greased 2-qt. baking dish.

Combine remaining bread crumbs and butter; sprinkle over casserole. Sprinkle with paprika. Bake, uncovered, at 425° for 16-18 minutes or until golden brown and edges are bubbly.

Yield: 4 servings.

Spinach Salad

A simple spinach salad complements this hearty crab casserole.

Combine 5 cups torn spinach, 1 cup sliced mushrooms and 1/2 cup thinly sliced red onion in a salad bowl. Drizzle with Catalina, French, Italian or Thousand Island salad dressing.

Tasty Term

Deviled is a generic term referring to highly seasoned foods.

Seafood Nachos

Prep/Total Time: 20 min.

30	baked tortilla chips
1	package (8 ounces) imitation crabmeat, chopped
1/4	cup sour cream
1/4	cup mayonnaise
2	tablespoons finely chopped onion
1/4	teaspoon dill weed
1	cup (4 ounces) shredded cheddar cheese
1/4	cup sliced ripe olives
1/4	teaspoon paprika

Arrange tortilla chips in a single layer on an ungreased baking sheet. In a bowl, combine the crab, sour cream, mayonnaise, onion and dill; spoon about 1 tablespoon onto each chip. Sprinkle with cheese, olives and paprika. Bake at 350° for 6-8 minutes or until cheese is melted.

Yield: 3 servings.

Dill Differences

Dill weed and dill seed come from the same plant. Dill weed refers to the dried leaves.

Dill weed and seed are not interchangeable. The seed has a slightly bitter taste and is suited for recipes like salad dressing.

Dill weed's delicate flavor enhances fish, seafood, vegetables and dip.

Preparation Pointer

You can find imitation crab (otherwise referred to as surimi) at the seafood counter of your local grocery store.

Fish Fillets with Stuffing

Prep/Total Time: 25 min.

2	tablespoons butter, melted
1/3	cup chicken broth
1/2	cup finely chopped onion
1/2	cup finely grated carrots
1/2	cup chopped fresh mushrooms
1/4	cup minced fresh parsley
1/2	cup dry bread crumbs
1	egg, beaten
1	tablespoon lemon juice
1	teaspoon salt
1/8	teaspoon pepper
2-1/2	to 3 pounds fish fillets (cod, whitefish, haddock, etc.)

Paprika

In a large bowl, combine the first 11 ingredients and mix well. In a greased 13-in. x 9-in. x 2-in. microwave-safe dish, arrange the fillets with stuffing between them. Moisten paper towels with water; place over fish. Cook 15-16 minutes or until fish flakes easily with a fork, rotating dish occasionally. Sprinkle with paprika.

Editor's Note: This recipe was tested in a 700-watt microwave.

Yield: 6-8 servings.

Microwave Meal

Cooking meals in the microwave works best for foods that have a high moisture content, like fish, poultry and vegetables.

No Bones About It

Before cooking fish, run your fingers gently over the fish to find any bones. Easily pull them out with clean kitchen pliers or tweezers.

Sesame Dill Fish

Prep/Total Time: 15 min.

1/2   **cup dry bread crumbs**
1/4   **cup sesame seeds**
1/2   **teaspoon dill weed**
1/4   **teaspoon salt**
3/4   **cup plain yogurt**
  1   **pound catfish** *or* **other whitefish fillets**
1/4   **cup vegetable oil**
Lemon wedges, optional

In a shallow bowl, combine bread crumbs, sesame seeds, dill and salt. Place yogurt in another bowl; stir until smooth. Dip fillets in yogurt; shake off excess, then dip in crumb mixture.

Heat oil in a large nonstick skillet. Fry fillets over medium-high heat for 2-3 minutes on each side or until fish flakes easily with a fork. Serve with lemon if desired.

Yield: 4 servings.

Homemade Bread Crumbs

Do you ever have leftover end pieces of bread that your family won't eat? Place them in a heavy-duty resealable plastic bag and freeze to make your own dry bread crumbs.

For 2 cups bread crumbs, place 8 pieces of bread in a single layer on a baking sheet. Bake in a 250° oven until very dry; let cool. Process the dry bread in a food processor until finely crushed.

For seasoned bread crumbs, add 1 teaspoon salt, 2 teaspoons paprika, 1 teaspoon celery salt, 1 teaspoon onion salt and 1/4 teaspoon pepper. Store in an airtight container.

Garlic Salmon Linguine

Prep/Total Time: 15 min.

1 package (16 ounces) linguine
3 garlic cloves, minced
1/3 cup olive oil
1 can (14-3/4 ounces) salmon,
     drained, bones and skin
     removed
3/4 cup chicken broth
1/4 cup minced fresh parsley
1/2 teaspoon salt
1/8 teaspoon cayenne pepper

Cook the linguine according to package directions. Meanwhile, in a large skillet, saute garlic in oil. Stir in the salmon, broth, parsley, salt and cayenne. Cook until heated through. Drain linguine; add to the salmon mixture and toss to coat.

Yield: 6 servings.

Sauteing Garlic

Watch garlic closely when sauteing so it doesn't burn. Cook garlic in oil on low heat, just long enough to make the garlic sizzle.

Seafood Substitute

For a seafood pasta dinner, replace the salmon with canned crabmeat and cooked shrimp.

New England Clam Chowder

Prep/Total Time: 15 min.

> 2 cans (10-3/4 ounces *each*) condensed New
>   England clam chowder, undiluted
> 2-2/3 cups milk
>   2 cans (6-1/2 ounces *each*) chopped clams, drained
> 1/4 cup sherry *or* chicken broth
>   2 tablespoons butter
> Shredded cheddar cheese, optional

In a saucepan, combine the first five ingredients. Bring to a boil.
Reduce heat; cover and simmer for 5 minutes. Garnish with cheese
if desired.

Yield: 6 servings.

Superior Sherry

Sherry adds a bit more complex flavor to this chowder than chicken broth. But don't use sherry labeled as a cooking wine.

Cooking wines, which are located near the bottled vinegars, are made with an inferior wine to which salt and food coloring have been added.

Instead, pick up a bottle of sherry from your store's wine department.

Nut-Crusted Fried Fish

Prep/Total Time: 20 min.

- 1/4 cup plus 2 tablespoons seasoned bread crumbs
- 1/4 cup plus 2 tablespoons finely chopped pecans *or* pistachios
- 1/2 teaspoon salt

Dash pepper

- 1/4 cup plus 2 tablespoons all-purpose flour
- 1/4 cup plus 2 tablespoons milk
- 1 pound fish fillets (about 1/2 inch thick)
- 1/4 cup vegetable oil

In a shallow bowl, combine the bread crumbs, pecans or pistachios, salt and pepper. Place the flour in a shallow bowl and the milk in another bowl. Cut the fish fillets into serving-size pieces if necessary.

Dredge fish in flour, dip in milk, then coat with the crumb mixture. Heat oil in a nonstick skillet over medium heat. Fry the fish for 4-5 minutes on each side or until it flakes easily with a fork.

Yield: 4 servings.

Spicy Coating

If your family is a fan of the flavor of pepper, replace the nutty crumb mixture with cracked peppercorns.

Fast Finishes

Frozen French fries and mixed vegetables are speedy sides to serve alongside these fish fillets.

Southwestern Fish Tacos

Prep/Total Time: 20 min.

1/2 cup sour cream
1/2 cup mayonnaise
1/4 cup minced fresh cilantro
8 teaspoons taco seasoning, *divided*
2 tablespoons lemon juice
1 pound cod, haddock *or* orange roughy fillets, cut into 1-inch pieces
2 tablespoons vegetable oil
8 taco shells

Optional toppings: shredded lettuce *or* cabbage, chopped tomatoes, lime juice and salsa

In a small bowl, combine the sour cream, mayonnaise, cilantro and 2 teaspoons taco seasoning; set aside.

In another bowl, combine the lemon juice and remaining taco seasoning. Add fish; toss to coat. In a small skillet, cook fish over medium-high heat in oil for about 6 minutes. (Fish will break apart as it cooks.) Fill taco shells with fish mixture. Serve with toppings of your choice. Serve with sour cream mixture.

Yield: 4 servings.

Cilantro Tips

Bunches of cilantro are available throughout the year. Look for fresh-looking leaves, avoiding any bunch that has begun to discolor or wilt.

At home, wash and dry it gently. To store, place the bunch, stem end down, in a small glass of water. Cover with a plastic bag and secure a rubber band around the glass. Change the water every day or so.

Seafood Alfredo

Prep/Total Time: 20 min.

1 package (12 ounces) bow tie pasta
2 garlic cloves, minced
2 tablespoons olive oil
1 package (8 ounces) imitation crabmeat, flaked
1 package (5 ounces) frozen cooked salad shrimp, thawed
1 tablespoon lemon juice
1/2 teaspoon pepper
1 jar (16 ounces) Alfredo sauce
1/2 cup frozen peas, thawed
1/4 cup shredded Parmesan cheese

Cook pasta according to package directions. Meanwhile, in a large skillet, saute garlic in oil until tender. Stir in the crab, shrimp, lemon juice and pepper. Cook and stir for 1 minute. Add Alfredo sauce and peas. Cook and stir until heated through. Drain pasta; top with the seafood mixture and sprinkle with Parmesan cheese.

Yield: 4-6 servings.

All About Alfredo

Alfredo sauce was created in 1914 by Roman restaurateur Alfredo di Lelio as a way for his expectant wife to regain her appetite.

Thawing Shrimp

Although frozen cooked shrimp can be thawed quickly in cold water, they'll have better flavor if defrosted in the refrigerator. So plan ahead when preparing this recipe.

Lemon Dill Walleye

Prep/Total Time: 30 min.

1 large onion, halved and thinly sliced
1 tablespoon butter
4 cups water
1 tablespoon snipped fresh dill *or* 1 teaspoon dill weed
3/4 cup milk
2 medium lemons, thinly sliced
1/8 teaspoon pepper
2 pounds walleye, code, halibut *or* orange roughy fillets

In a large skillet, saute onion in butter until tender. Add water and dill; bring to a boil. Reduce heat; simmer, uncovered, for 4-5 minutes. Add milk; stir in lemons and pepper. Top with fillets. Cover and simmer for 12-15 minutes or until fish flakes easily with a fork.

Transfer fish to a serving platter and keep warm. Strain cooking liquid, reserving lemons, onion and dill; serve with fish.

Yield: 8 servings.

Fresh Dill Facts

Fresh dill can be found in grocery stores all year long. Wrap fresh dill loosely in a plastic bag and store in the refrigerator for 3 to 4 days.

Walleye Lesson

Walleye is a freshwater fish with firm flesh that is mild in flavor and low in fat.

Microwave Tuna Casserole

Prep/Total Time: 20 min.

1/2 cup sour cream
1/2 cup mayonnaise
  2 teaspoons prepared
    mustard
1/2 teaspoon salt
1/2 teaspoon dried thyme
1/4 teaspoon dill weed
  5 cups cooked egg noodles
  2 cans (6 ounces *each*) tuna,
    drained and flaked
1/2 cup chopped celery
1/3 cup sliced green onions
  1 small zucchini, sliced
  1 cup (4 ounces) shredded cheddar cheese
  1 medium tomato, chopped

In a small bowl, combine the first six ingredients; mix well. In a large bowl, combine noodles, tuna, celery and onions. Stir in the sour cream mixture. Spoon half into a greased 2-qt. microwave-safe dish; top with half of the zucchini. Repeat layers.

Microwave, uncovered, on high for 6-8 minutes or until heated through. Sprinkle with cheese and tomato. Microwave, uncovered, 2 minutes longer. Let stand for 3 minutes before serving.

Editor's Note: This recipe was tested in an 850-watt microwave.

Yield: 6 servings.

Preparation Pointer

A 16-ounce package of un-cooked egg noodles is roughly equivalent to 5 cups cooked.

Time-Saving Tip

Make this dinner in a dash by doing some prep work the night before.
  Cook and drain the egg noodles and place in a re-sealable plastic bag. Close bag and refrigerate.
  Chop the celery and slice the green onions and zucchini. Store in separate covered containers; chill.

Basil Walnut Fish Fillets

Prep/Total Time: 20 min.

1-1/2 pounds fresh *or* frozen cod *or* haddock fillets
  3 tablespoons mayonnaise
  2 tablespoons sour cream
  2 tablespoons grated Parmesan cheese
  1 tablespoon minced fresh basil *or* 1 teaspoon dried basil
1/4 cup chopped walnuts

Cut fish into serving-size pieces and place in a greased 13-in. x 9-in. x 2-in. baking dish. Combine the mayonnaise, sour cream, Parmesan cheese and basil; spread over fish. Sprinkle with walnuts. Bake, uncovered, at 425° for 10-15 minutes or until fish flakes easily with a fork.

Yield: 4 servings.

Simple Side Dish

A simple side liked cooked carrots adds color to the plate.

In a skillet, saute 3 cups julienned carrots in 1 tablespoon oil for 3 minutes. Add 1/2 cup sliced green onions; cook 4-5 minutes longer or until crisp-tender.

Stir in 1 tablespoon lemon juice, 3/4 teaspoon Italian seasoning, 1/2 teaspoon garlic salt and a dash of pepper.

Seafood Pasta

Prep/Total Time: 25 min.

> 4 garlic cloves, minced
> 1/4 cup butter, *divided*
> 6 plum tomatoes, chopped
> 4 teaspoons minced fresh parsley
> 4 teaspoons minced fresh basil *or* 1/2 teaspoon dried basil
> 1/4 to 1/2 teaspoon dried tarragon
> 1-1/2 cups chicken broth
> 8 ounces thin spaghetti
> 1/2 pound uncooked medium shrimp, peeled and deveined
> 1/2 pound bay scallops
> Shredded Parmesan cheese, optional

In a medium skillet, saute 2 garlic cloves in 2 tablespoon butter for 1 minute. Add the tomatoes, parsley, basil and tarragon; saute 2 minutes longer. Add the broth; bring to a boil. Reduce heat; simmer, uncovered, for 8-10 minutes or until mixture reaches desired thickness.

Meanwhile, cook pasta according to package directions. In another skillet, saute remaining garlic in remaining butter for 1 minute. Add shrimp; cook and stir for 1 minute. Add scallops and cook 3 minutes longer or until shrimp turn pink and scallops are firm and opaque. Add to tomato mixture. Drain pasta; transfer to a bowl. Pour seafood mixture over pasta; toss to coat. Sprinkle with Parmesan if desired.

Yield: 4 servings.

Easy Substitution

If you prefer, use 1 pound of shrimp and leave out the scallops.

Scallop Secrets

Bay scallops are smaller in size than sea scallops and are tender and sweeter in flavor.

The color of fresh scallops can range from pale beige to creamy pink. Cook fresh scallops within 1 day. Frozen scallops should be used within 3 months.

Triple-Decker Salmon Club

Prep/Total Time: 15 min.

 1-1/2   cups small-curd cottage cheese
 1/2   cup dill pickle relish
 2   cans (6 ounces *each*) salmon, drained, bones and skin removed
 2   celery ribs, chopped
 12   slices bread, toasted
 24   lettuce leaves, optional

In a small bowl, combine cottage cheese and pickle relish. In another bowl, combine salmon and celery. For each sandwich, top one piece of toast with lettuce if desired and half of the cottage cheese mixture. Top with a second piece of toast; spread with half of the salmon mixture. Top with a third piece of toast.

Yield: 4 servings.

Lively Leftover

Next time you make a fresh salmon fillet for dinner, double the recipe. Use some of the leftovers to replace the canned salmon in this sandwich.

Simple Substitution

For a tasty twist, substitute smoked salmon for the canned salmon.

Any kind of bread can be used in this recipe. Try English muffin, whole wheat, oatmeal or sourdough.

Italian Catfish Fillets

Prep/Total Time: 30 min.

1   **can (8 ounces) tomato sauce**
2   **teaspoons olive oil**
1   **teaspoon zesty Italian
    salad dressing mix**
1/4   **teaspoon salt**
1/8   **teaspoon pepper**
4   **catfish fillets (6 ounces *each*)**
3   **tablespoons shredded
    Romano cheese**

In a bowl, combine the first five ingredients. Pour half of the sauce into an 11-in. x 7-in. x 2-in. baking dish coated with nonstick cooking spray. Arrange fish over sauce. Top with remaining sauce. Bake, uncovered, at 375° for 20 minutes. Sprinkle with cheese. Bake 5 minutes longer or until fish flakes easily with a fork and cheese is melted.

Yield: 4 servings.

Catfish Facts

A 3-1/2-ounce serving of farm-raised catfish contains 15 grams of protein, 7 grams of fat, 33 milligrams of cholesterol, 33 milligrams of sodium and 128 calories.

Timely Tip

For an even faster recipe, use prepared spaghetti sauce for the tomato sauce and seasonings.

Crispy Catfish

Prep/Total Time: 15 min.

3/4 cup finely crushed saltines (about 22 crackers)

1 teaspoon seasoned salt

1/2 teaspoon celery salt

1/2 teaspoon garlic salt

4 catfish fillets (about 8 ounces *each*)

1/3 cup butter, melted

In a shallow dish, combine the first four ingredients. Pat fillets dry; dip in butter, then coat with crumb mixture. Coat grill rack with nonstick cooking spray before starting grill. Grill fillets, covered, over medium-hot heat for 10 minutes or until fish flakes easily with a fork, carefully turning once.

Yield: 4 servings.

Grilled Veggies

Julienne 1 small zucchini, 1 small yellow summer squash and 1 small carrot. Chop 1 small onion. Place vegetables in a foil bag. Dot with 2 tablespoons butter; season with salt, pepper and garlic powder. Seal bag tightly.

Grill, covered, over medium heat for 14-16 minutes or until tender, turning once. Sprinkle with 2 tablespoons grated Parmesan cheese and 2 tablespoons shredded mozzarella.

Shrimp Marinara

Prep: 30 min.   **Cook:** 3 hours 20 min.

  1 **can (14-1/2 ounces) Italian diced tomatoes,
     undrained**
  1 **can (6 ounces) tomato paste**
1/2 **to 1 cup water**
  2 **garlic cloves, minced**
  2 **tablespoons minced fresh parsley**
  1 **teaspoon salt**
  1 **teaspoon dried oregano**
1/2 **teaspoon dried basil**
1/4 **teaspoon pepper**
  1 **pound fresh *or* frozen shrimp, cooked, peeled and
     deveined**
  1 **pound spaghetti, cooked and drained**
Shredded Parmesan cheese, optional

In a slow cooker, combine the first nine ingredients. Cover and
cook on low for 3-4 hours. Stir in shrimp. Cover and cook 20 minutes longer or just until shrimp are heated through. Serve over
spaghetti. Garnish with Parmesan cheese if desired.

Yield: 6 servings.

Delicious Bread

Discover how easy it is to
make restaurant-style
bread at home! Just slice
some crusty French bread
and serve along with olive
oil for dipping.

   If desired, add a drop or
two of balsamic vinegar in
the oil and sprinkle with
grated Parmesan cheese.

Timely Tip

By keeping a bag of frozen
cooked shrimp in the freezer, you can make this saucy
supper anytime. There's no
need to thaw the shrimp
before adding to the slow
cooker.

Fish in Foil

Prep/Total Time: 25 min.

1 halibut steak (6 ounces)
4 medium mushrooms
2 cherry tomatoes, halved
2 lemon slices
1/2 medium green pepper,
  sliced
1/4 cup diet Mountain Dew
Crushed pepper

Place fish in the center of a 20-in. x 14-in. piece of heavy-duty foil. Place mushrooms, tomatoes, lemon and green pepper around fish. Fold edges of oil up; pour soda over fish. Fold foil to seal tightly. Bake at 375° for 20-25 minutes or until fish flakes easily with a fork. Open foil carefully to allow steam to escape. Sprinkle with pepper.

Yield: 1 serving.

Halibut Hint

Look for halibut steaks with pure white flesh and a slightly sweet smell. Don't buy halibut that is brown and dry.

The edible skin doesn't need to be removed before cooking. In fact, leaving the skin intact helps the halibut keep its shape.

Preparation Pointer

This recipe can easily be increased to feed a family. Make a foil pouch for everyone and have them assemble their own packet.

Crabby Bagels

Prep/Total Time: 15 min.

1   can (6 ounces) crabmeat, drained, flaked and cartilage removed

1/2 cup shredded cheddar cheese

1/4 cup finely chopped celery

1/4 cup sour cream

3/4 teaspoon Worcestershire sauce

1/4 teaspoon salt

4   onion bagels, split

1   package (3 ounces) cream cheese, softened

4   lettuce leaves

In a bowl, combine the first six ingredients. Toast bagels; spread with cream cheese. On the bottom of each bagel, place a lettuce leaf and 1/4 cup of crab mixture. Replace tops.

Yield: 4 servings.

Play with Your Food!

The best way to remove cartilage and any small pieces of shell from canned crabmeat is by using your fingers.

Serving Suggestion

If you're looking for a low-carb option, serve the crab mixture on a bed of lettuce. Top with additional vegetables if you like.

Lemon Shrimp Ravioli Toss

Prep/Total Time: 15 min.

      3 **cups refrigerated cheese ravioli**
    1/4 **cup butter, melted**
      2 **tablespoons lemon juice**
  1-1/2 **teaspoons snipped fresh basil**
      1 **teaspoon grated lemon peel**
  2-2/3 **cups cooked medium shrimp,**
        peeled and deveined

Cook ravioli according to package directions; drain. In a microwave-safe 1-qt. dish,
combine the butter, lemon juice, basil and
lemon peel. Add shrimp and ravioli; toss to
coat. Cover and microwave on high for 2-4
minutes or until heated through.

Editor's Note: This recipe was tested in an 850-watt microwave.

Yield: 2 servings.

Rapid Ravioli

Frozen ravioli can be used
in place of the refrigerated
ravioli. It will just need to
cook a bit longer.

Shrimp Pointers

A half-pound of shrimp
equals about 1/2 cup. So
pick up 1 to 1-1/2 pounds
cooked shrimp from the
grocery store for this recipe.

Cooked shrimp can be
stored in a sealed bag for
up to 3 days in the coldest
part of your refrigerator.

Halibut Steaks

Prep/Total Time: 20 min.

1/2 **cup soy sauce**

1/4 **cup packed brown sugar**

2 **garlic cloves, minced**

1/8 **teaspoon pepper**

Dash hot pepper sauce

Pinch dried oregano

Pinch dried basil

4 **halibut steaks (6 ounces *each*)**

1/2 **cup chopped onion**

4 **lemon slices**

4 **teaspoons butter**

In a small bowl, combine the first seven ingredients. Place each halibut steak on a double thickness of heavy-duty foil (about 18 in. x 12 in.); top with soy sauce mixture, onion, lemon and butter. Fold foil around fish and seal tightly. Grill, covered, over medium heat for 10-14 minutes or until fish flakes easily with a fork.

Yield: 4 servings.

Cooking Fish

Because fish is low in fat, it can become tough and dry if overcooked. So remove it from the heat as soon as it loses the translucent appearance in the center

Use the "10-minute rule" to estimate cooking time for fish. Measure the fish at its thickest part. Allow about 10 minutes of cooking time for each inch of thickness.

Pineapple-Glazed Fish

Prep/Total Time: 25 min.

>   1 can (8 ounces) unsweetened sliced pineapple
> 1-1/2 teaspoons cornstarch
>   1/4 teaspoon ground ginger
>   2 tablespoons honey
>   2 tablespoons soy sauce
>   1 tablespoon lemon juice
>   4 orange roughy *or* haddock fillets (6 ounces *each*)

Drain pineapple, reserving juice; set pineapple aside. In a small saucepan, combine the cornstarch and ginger; stir in pineapple juice until blended. Add the honey and soy sauce. Bring to a boil; cook and stir for 1-2 minutes or until thickened. Stir in lemon juice. Pour half into a small bowl for serving.

Coat grill rack with nonstick cooking spray before starting the grill. Grill fillets, uncovered, over medium heat for 4-5 minutes. Spoon some of the glaze over fillets. Cook 4-5 minutes. Spoon some of the glaze over fillets. Cook 4-5 minutes longer or until fish flakes easily with a fork.

Meanwhile, grill pineapple slices for 4-6 minutes or until heated through, basting frequently with glaze and turning once. Serve fish with pineapple and reserved glaze.

Yield: 4 servings.

Orange Roughy Facts

Orange roughy is an all-purpose white-fleshed fish. The meat is firm, low in fat and mild in flavor. Other whitefish fillets include ocean perch, cod, haddock, pollock and red snapper.

Timely Tip

Whip up the pineapple sauce for this recipe earlier in the day or even the night before. Transfer to a covered container; chill.

Fried Fish Nuggets

Prep/Total Time: 25 min.

2 eggs, beaten
1/2 cup dry bread crumbs
1/2 cup shredded cheddar cheese
1/4 cup finely chopped onion
1 garlic clove, minced
1-1/2 teaspoons minced fresh parsley
1/4 teaspoon dill weed
1/4 teaspoon pepper
1-1/2 cups flaked cooked fish
Oil for deep-fat frying
Tartar sauce, optional

In a bowl, combine the first eight ingredients; mix well. Stir in the fish. Roll into 1-in. balls. Heat oil in a deep-fat fryer to 375°. Fry fish nuggets for 2 minutes or until golden brown; drain on paper towels. Serve with tartar sauce if desired.

Yield: about 2-1/2 dozen.

Deep-Frying Facts

Carefully place foods into hot oil to avoid splattering.

You'll have better results if you fry in small batches. Keep cooked foods in a warm oven until all the food has been fried.

Preparation Pointer

Is your family not fond of leftovers? Turn chunks of leftover fish into these tasty nuggets!

Round out your weeknight meals with an assortment of garden-fresh veggies, satisfying grains, hearty breads and cool salads.

Zesty Vegetable Skewers
(p. 289)

Swift Sides & Salads

Apple Spinach Salad (p. 283)

Italian Vegetable Saute

Prep/Total Time: 15 min.

 2 medium green peppers, sliced
 1 garlic clove, minced
 1 teaspoon Italian seasoning
 1 tablespoon butter
 1 cup cherry tomatoes, halved
 1/2 cup seasoned croutons, optional

In a skillet, saute the peppers, garlic and Italian seasoning in butter until peppers are crisp-tender, about 5 minutes. Add tomatoes; cook for 1-2 minutes or until heated through. Sprinkle with croutons if desired.

Yield: 4 servings.

Simple Substitution

If you don't have fresh garlic on hand, you can substitute 1/8 teaspoon garlic powder for one garlic clove.

Timely Tip

Save a bit of time when preparing this recipe by keeping the cherry tomatoes whole instead of cutting them in half.

Parmesan Chicken (p. 90)

Penne from Heaven

Prep/Total Time: 25 min.

  6 ounces uncooked penne *or* other small pasta
1/2 pound fresh mushrooms, sliced
  1 tablespoon olive oil
  1 can (14-1/2 ounces) diced tomatoes, undrained
  1 tablespoon minced fresh basil *or* 1 teaspoon dried
     basil
1/4 teaspoon salt
1/3 cup crumbled feta cheese

Cook pasta according to package directions. Meanwhile, in a large skillet, saute mushrooms in oil for 5 minutes. Add the tomatoes, basil and salt; cook and stir for 5 minutes. Drain pasta and add to the skillet. Stir in the cheese; heat through.

Yield: 5 servings.

Mushroom Secrets

Buy already-sliced mushrooms for this recipe.

Mushrooms are best when used within several days after purchase. Place in a paper bag and refrigerate. Storing in air-tight containers or plastic bags will cause condensation and speed spoilage.

Serving Suggestion

For a light meal, serve this delicious pasta dish with a green salad and toasted garlic bread.

Romaine with Oranges and Almonds

Prep/Total Time: 10 min.

> 8 cups torn romaine
> 1 can (11 ounces) mandarin oranges, drained
> 2 green onions, thinly sliced
> 1/4 cup slivered almonds, toasted
> 1/4 cup sugar
> 1/4 cup vegetable oil
> 1/4 cup white vinegar

In a bowl, toss the first four ingredients. In a jar with a tight-fitting lid, combine sugar, oil and vinegar; shake well. Drizzle over salad and toss to coat.

Yield: 8 servings.

Romaine Rules

Romaine lettuce has deep green, long leaves with a crisp texture. The head should be compact and the leaves should be free of bruises and blemishes.

When you bring romaine home from the store, wash and dry it. (A salad spinner is an excellent, inexpensive tool to have on hand.)

Store in a plastic bag or wrap in a damp cloth and place in the refrigerator crisper.

Romaine lettuce will keep for 5 to 7 days.

Steamed Lemon Broccoli

Prep/Total Time: 20 min.

1 large bunch broccoli, cut
   into spears
1 medium onion, halved and
   thinly sliced
1 cup thinly sliced celery
3 garlic cloves, minced
3 tablespoons butter
2 teaspoons grated lemon peel
1-1/2 teaspoons lemon juice
1/2 teaspoon salt
1/4 teaspoon pepper

In a saucepan, bring 1 in. of water to a boil; place broccoli in a steamer basket over the water. Cover; steam for 5-6 minutes or until crisp-tender. Rinse in cold water; drain and set aside.

In a skillet, saute the onion, celery and garlic in butter until vegetables are tender, about 5 minutes. Add the lemon peel and juice, salt if desired, pepper and broccoli; heat through.

Yield: 4 servings.

Broccoli Basics

Look for bunches of fresh broccoli with firm yet tender stalks that have compact, dark green or slightly purplish florets.

Keep unwashed broccoli in an open plastic bag in the crisper drawer for up to 4 days.

Wash broccoli and remove larger leaves and tough ends of lower stalks. If using whole spears, cut lengthwise into 1-in.-wide pieces.

A pound of broccoli serves 3 to 4 people.

Great Garden Veggies

Prep/Total Time: 15 min.

> 1 medium zucchini, cut into 1/4-inch slices
> 1 medium yellow summer squash, cut into 1/4-inch slices
> 1/4 cup sliced onion
> 1 tablespoon butter
> 1 medium tomato, cut into wedges
> 1/4 teaspoon salt
> 1/4 teaspoon garlic salt
> 1/4 teaspoon dried basil
> 1/4 teaspoon pepper
> 2 tablespoons grated Parmesan cheese

In a skillet, saute the zucchini, yellow squash and onion in butter until crisp tender. Add the tomato, salt, garlic salt, basil and pepper. Cook 2-3 minutes longer. Sprinkle with Parmesan cheese.

Yield: 4 servings.

Serving Suggestion

Turn this recipe into a meatless meal by tossing in hot cooked pasta. Or add some cubed cooked chicken or turkey for a more hearty dinner.

Timely Tip

You can slice the zucchini, yellow squash and onion in advance. Store in an airtight container and refrigerate overnight.

Grilled Peppered Steaks (p. 62)

Italian Rice

Prep/Total Time: 15 min.

2 garlic cloves, minced

2 teaspoons olive oil

8 cups fresh spinach (about 10 ounces), chopped

1 tablespoon balsamic vinegar

1/2 teaspoon salt

1/8 teaspoon pepper

2 cups hot cooked rice

1/2 cup chopped roasted sweet red peppers

In a large nonstick skillet, saute garlic in oil for 1 minute. Stir in spinach. Cover and cook for 3-4 minutes or until tender; drain well. Add the vinegar, salt and pepper. Stir in the rice and red peppers until combined. Cook and stir until heated through.

Yield: 4 servings.

Rice Equivalents

One cup instant rice will yield 2 cups cooked. One cup converted rice equals about 3-1/2 cups cooked. One cup brown rice yields about 4 cups cooked.

Roasted Peppers

Slightly smoky red peppers highlight this rice side dish. Look for jars of roasted red peppers in the condiments aisle.

Asparagus Linguine

Prep/Total Time: 25 min.

6 ounces uncooked linguine
1 small onion, chopped
2 garlic cloves, minced
1 tablespoon olive
2 teaspoons butter
1/2 pound fresh asparagus, trimmed and cut into 1/2-inch pieces
2 tablespoons white wine *or* chicken broth
2 tablespoons grated Parmesan cheese
1 tablespoon lemon juice
1/4 teaspoon salt
1/8 teaspoon pepper

Cook linguine according to package directions. Meanwhile, in a nonstick skillet, saute the onion and garlic in oil and butter until tender. Add asparagus; cook and stir for 2 minutes or until crisp-tender. Add wine or broth; cook and stir for 1-2 minutes or until liquid is reduced. Remove from the heat.

Drain linguine; add to asparagus mixture. Add remaining ingredients; toss to coat.

Yield: 4 servings.

Pasta Tip

Linguine is sold in 16-ounce packages, but you only need 6 ounces for this recipe. Here's a trick for measuring what you need.

Eight ounces of linguine is about 1-1/2 inches in diameter. So for 6 ounces, take slightly less than that.

Place the leftover uncooked linguine in an airtight container or resealable plastic bag. Use it to make Pepper Beef Stir-Fry (p. 76) or Linguine with Fresh Tomatoes (p. 210).

Parmesan Garlic Bread

Prep/Total Time: 25 min.

- 1/4 cup butter, softened
- 1/4 cup olive oil
- 1/4 cup grated Parmesan cheese
- 2 garlic cloves
- 4 sprigs fresh parsley
- 1/2 teaspoon lemon-pepper seasoning
- 1 small loaf (8 ounces) French bread

In a mixing bowl or food processor, blend butter, oil and Parmesan cheese. Add garlic, parsley and lemon-pepper; mix or process until smooth.

Slice the bread on the diagonal but not all the way through, leaving slices attached at the bottom. Spread butter mixture on one side of each slice and over the top. Wrap in foil and bake at 400° for 15-20 minutes.

Yield: 4 servings.

Grilled Garlic Bread

If you're preparing your entree on the grill, why not barbecue this bread as well?

Grill the foil-wrapped bread over medium heat for 8-10 minutes, turning once.

If you want crisp bread, unwrap the foil and grill 5 minutes longer.

Preparation Pointer

You can double the recipe for this bread's garlic butter and freeze half for a future meal.

Feta-Topped Asparagus

Prep/Total Time: 15 min.

1-1/2 pounds fresh asparagus
   1 medium red onion, sliced and separated into rings
   2 tablespoons olive oil
Salt and pepper to taste
  1/4 cup crumbled feta cheese

Place 1/2 in. of water and the asparagus in a large skillet; bring to a boil. Reduce heat; cover and simmer for 3-5 minutes or until crisp-tender; drain. Remove asparagus and keep warm. Saute onion in oil until crisp-tender. Return asparagus to the pan. Sprinkle with salt, pepper and cheese.

Yield: 4 servings.

Cooking Asparagus

For even cooking, buy asparagus spears that are roughly the same size and thickness.

Before cooking asparagus, soak the stalks in cold water to clean. Snap off the stalk ends as far down as they will easily break when gently bent.

Feta Facts

Feta is a white, salty, semi-firm cheese. Traditionally, it was made from sheep or goat's milk but is now also made with cow's milk.

Italian Pineapple Chicken (p. 94)

Creamy Hash Browns

Prep: 10 min.   **Cook:** 4 hours

- 1 package (2 pounds) frozen cubed hash brown potatoes
- 2 cups (8 ounces) cubed *or* shredded process cheese (Velveeta)
- 2 cups (16 ounces) sour cream
- 1 can (10-3/4 ounces) condensed cream of celery soup, undiluted
- 1 can (10-3/4 ounces) condensed cream of chicken soup, undiluted
- 1 pound sliced bacon, cooked and crumbled
- 1 large onion, chopped
- 1/4 cup butter, melted
- 1/4 teaspoon pepper

Place potatoes in an ungreased 5-qt. slow cooker. In a bowl, combine the remaining ingredients. Pour over potatoes and mix well. Cover and cook on low for 4-5 hours or until potatoes are tender and heated through.

Yield: 14 servings.

Party Hearty

This potato dish serves a group, making it perfect for parties. Try this easy entree to pair it with.

In a bowl, combine one 16-ounce bottle of Catalina salad dressing, 2/3 cup apricot preserves and two envelopes onion soup mix. Place 16 boneless skinless chicken breast halves in two ungreased 11-in. x 7-in. x 2-in. baking pans; top with dressing mixture.

Cover and bake at 350° for 20 minutes; baste. Bake, uncovered, 20 minutes more or until chicken juices run clear.

Colorful Couscous

Prep/Total Time: 25 min.

1/3 cup *each* finely chopped onion, green pepper and sweet red pepper
2 garlic cloves, minced
2 tablespoons olive oil
1 can (14-1/2 ounces) chicken broth
1/4 cup water
1/2 teaspoon salt
1/4 teaspoon pepper
1 package (10 ounces) couscous

In a large saucepan, saute the onion, peppers and garlic in oil for 3 minutes. Stir in the broth, water, salt and pepper. Bring to a boil. Stir in the couscous. Cover and remove from the heat; let stand for 5 minutes. Fluff with a fork.

Yield: 6 servings.

A Course in Couscous

Couscous is a coarsely ground semolina pasta that has been a staple in many North African countries for centuries.

Nowadays, Americans are reaching for this quick-cooking grain more and more.

Look for both plain and flavored couscous near the rice mixes at your grocery store. Experiment with different varieties when making this side dish.

Stir-Fried Cabbage

Prep/Total Time: 15 min.

    2 tablespoons vegetable oil
    6 cups sliced cabbage
    3 tablespoons water
  1/2 teaspoon salt

In a large skillet, heat oil over medium heat. Add the cabbage, water and salt. Cook, uncovered, for 5-7 minutes or until cabbage is crisp-tender, stirring occasionally.

Yield: 4 servings.

Main-Dish Idea

Turn this into an easy entree by adding leftover pork tenderloin to the skillet toward the end of the cooking time and heating through.

Preparation Pointers

Have fun by varying the flavor of this versatile side dish.

Sprinkle in some Cajun seasoning or crushed red pepper flakes. Make Chinese-style cabbage by adding soy sauce.

Cabbage gets Old-World flavor when combined with chopped onion and apple.

Or for a creamy version, add a 3-ounce package of cubed, softened cream cheese; stir until melted.

Broiled Ginger Chicken (p. 85)

Basil Brussels Sprouts

Prep/Total Time: 15 min.

2 pounds Brussels sprouts, trimmed and halved
3 tablespoons water
1/4 cup butter, melted
1/2 teaspoon salt
1/2 teaspoon dried basil
1/2 teaspoon pepper

Place the Brussels sprouts and water in a 2-qt. microwave-safe dish. Cover and microwave on high for 6-8 minutes or until crisp-tender; drain. Combine the butter, salt, basil and pepper; drizzle over Brussels sprouts and toss to coat.

Editor's Note: This recipe was tested in an 850-watt microwave.

Yield: 4-6 servings.

Brussels Sprouts Basics

Buy small, firm, tightly closed heads that have bright green color.

Keep unwashed Brussels sprouts in an open plastic bag in the crisper drawer for up to 2 days.

Before using, remove any loose or yellow outer leaves; trim stem end. Rinse the sprouts.

If cooking the sprouts whole, cut an "X" in the stem end with a sharp knife.

Zucchini and Corn Saute

Prep/Total Time: 15 min.

2   **medium zucchini, thinly sliced**
1   **medium green pepper, thinly sliced**
1   **medium sweet red pepper, thinly sliced**
2   **to 3 tablespoons vegetable oil**
2   **cups fresh *or* frozen corn**
1   **teaspoon garlic salt**
1/2 **teaspoon Italian seasoning**

In a large skillet, saute zucchini and peppers in oil until crisp-tender, about 4 minutes in oil until crisp-tender, about 4 minutes. Add remaining ingredients; saute 3-4 minutes longer or until the corn is tender.

Yield: 10 servings.

Preparation Pointer

Although this recipe tastes just great with frozen corn, reach for fresh corn on the cob in summer.

To remove the kernels from the cobs, stand one end of the cob on a cutting board. Starting at the top, run a sharp knife down the cob, cutting deeply to remove whole kernels.

One medium cob yields about 1/2 cup of kernels.

Cool Cucumber Salad

Prep/Total Time: 30 min.

    1   medium cucumber, quartered
        and sliced
    1   medium tomato, chopped
  1/2   cup chopped green pepper
  1/3   cup chopped sweet onion
    2   tablespoons lime juice
    2   tablespoons red wine vinegar
  3/4   teaspoon dill weed
  1/2   teaspoon salt
  1/4   teaspoon pepper

In a large bowl, combine the cucumber, tomato, green pepper and onion. In a small bowl, combine lime juice, vinegar, dill, salt and pepper. Pour over cucumber mixture; toss to coat. Cover and refrigerate for 15 minutes. Serve with a slotted spoon.

Yield: 4 servings.

Onion Know-How

When making this cool, crisp salad, be sure to use a sweet onion, such as Vidalia, Walla Walla, Bermuda, Texas Spring Sweet or Imperial Sweet. Other onions can have a little more bite that would overpower the flavor.

Sweet onions have thin, light skins and both a high water and sugar content, which means they also have a shorter shelf life than more bitter varieties.

One small onion equals 1/3 cup chopped.

Basil Cherry Tomatoes

Prep/Total Time: 10 min.

    3 pints cherry tomatoes, halved
  1/2 cup chopped fresh basil
1-1/2 teaspoons olive oil
Salt and pepper to taste
Lettuce leaves, optional

In a bowl, combine the tomatoes, basil, oil, salt and pepper. Cover and refrigerate until serving. Serve on lettuce if desired.

Yield: 4-6 servings.

Timely Tip

If you're pressed for time, you can leave the cherry tomatoes whole.

Windowsill Garden

If you like to cook with fresh herbs, buying them every time you need them can get expensive. So why not keep some potted herbs in your kitchen? Decide what herbs you cook with most often. Then buy those plants and set them in a sunny window. If you want, you can transplant the herbs to an outdoor garden when the weather allows.

Bacon Cheeseburger Pasta (p. 30)

Tomato Pizza Bread

Prep/Total Time: 30 min.

- 1 tube (10 ounces) refrigerated pizza crust
- 2 garlic cloves, minced
- 1/2 teaspoon dried oregano
- 1 cup (4 ounces) shredded mozzarella cheese, *divided*
- 1 plum tomato, halved lengthwise and thinly sliced
- 1/2 teaspoon Italian seasoning, optional

On a greased baking sheet, roll pizza crust into a 12-in. x 8-in. rectangle. Bake at 425° for 6-8 minutes or until the edges are lightly browned.

Sprinkle with garlic, oregano and half of the cheese. Arrange tomato slices in a single layer over cheese. Top with remaining cheese and Italian seasoning if desired. Bake 6-8 minutes longer or until cheese is melted and crust is lightly browned.

Yield: 8 servings.

Italian Twist

Spread some prepared pesto on the baked pizza crust before adding the other toppings.

Seafood Fare

Turn this into a hearty appetizer or light meal by sprinkling chopped cooked shrimp on top.

Zesty Sugar Snap Peas

Prep/Total Time: 15 min.

1 pound fresh *or* frozen sugar snap peas
1/2 cup water
1 tablespoon butter
1 garlic clove, minced
3/4 teaspoon lemon-pepper seasoning
1/4 teaspoon salt

In a skillet, bring peas and water to a boil. Reduce heat. Cover and cook for 6-7 minutes or until tender; drain. Add the remaining ingredients. Cook and stir for 2-3 minutes or until well-coated.

Yield: 4 servings.

Sugar Snap Pea Pointers

Look for sugar snap peas that are plump, crisp and bright green. The peas inside should be prominent. Avoid pods that are limp or broken.

Store unwashed snap peas in a plastic bag in the refrigerator for up to 3 days. Wash before using; remove the string if desired.

Squash and Pepper Skillet

Prep/Total Time: 25 min.

  1 **medium onion, thinly sliced**
  1 **tablespoon olive oil**
  5 **medium zucchini, sliced**
  3 **medium yellow summer squash, sliced**
  1 **small sweet red *or* green pepper, julienned**
  1 **garlic clove, minced**
Salt and pepper to taste

In a skillet, saute onion in oil until tender. Add the zucchini, yellow squash, red pepper and garlic; stir-fry for 12-15 minutes or until vegetables are crisp-tender. Season with salt and pepper.

Yield: 8 servings.

Preparation Pointer

Adjust the seasonings in this recipe to suit your family's taste and to go with the entree you're serving it with.

Sprinkle on Italian seasoning if pairing this dish with grilled Italian sausages.

When making fish, sprinkle the vegetables with lemon-pepper seasoning.

Timely Tip

If you slice the onion, zucchini, squash and pepper the night before, preparation of this simple side dish is even faster at dinnertime.

Topped Taters

Prep/Total Time: 30 min.

3 cups leftover mashed potatoes
3/4 cup sour cream, *divided*
3 tablespoons sliced green onions with tops, *divided*
1/4 to 1/2 teaspoon garlic salt
1/2 cup shredded cheddar cheese

Combine the potatoes, 1/4 cup sour cream, 1 tablespoon green onions and the garlic salt; mix well. Spoon into a greased 1-qt. baking dish.

Cover and bake at 350° for 20 minutes. Uncover; spread with the remaining sour cream. Sprinkle with cheese and remaining onions. Bake 5 minutes longer or until the cheese is melted.

Yield: 4 servings.

Helpful Hint

Keep this recipe in mind for Monday after you make a batch of mashed potatoes for dinner some Saturday or Sunday night.

If you don't have leftovers, use instant, refrigerated or frozen mashed potatoes instead.

Serving Suggestion

These mild, creamy potatoes would pair well with any entree, from pork and poultry to beef and fish.

Herbed Potato Wedges

Prep/Total Time: 30 min.

1-1/4	**pounds medium red potatoes**
2	**teaspoons butter**
2	**teaspoons lemon juice**
1/4	**cup grated Parmesan cheese**
1	**teaspoon dried thyme**
1/2	**teaspoon salt**
1/4	**teaspoon pepper**

Cut potatoes into quarters. In a bowl, combine butter and lemon juice; brush over cut surfaces of potatoes. Combine the remaining ingredients; dip coated sides of potatoes into cheese mixture. Place potatoes, cut sides up, in a 2-qt. microwave-safe dish. Cover and microwave on high for 12-15 minutes or until potatoes are tender.

Editor's Note: This recipe was tested in an 850-watt microwave.

Yield: 4 servings.

Tater Tips

Red potatoes are medium sized with thin, edible skin and flesh that has a crisp, waxy texture. The flesh can have a pink tint but is generally white.

If you buy potatoes in a plastic bag, put them in a basket or sack at home so they get air circulation. Store potatoes in a cool, dark place for up to 2 weeks.

Noodle Rice Pilaf

Prep/Total Time: 30 min.

1/4 cup butter
1 cup long grain rice
1/2 cup uncooked fine egg noodles
   or vermicelli
2-3/4 cups chicken broth
2 tablespoons minced fresh parsley

In a saucepan, melt butter. Add the rice and noodles; cook and stir until lightly browned, about 3 minutes. Stir in broth; bring to a boil. Reduce heat; cover and simmer for 20-25 minutes or until broth is absorbed and rice is tender. Stir in parsley.

Yield: 4 servings.

Preparing Pilaf

Sauteing the rice and noodles before cooking brings out a slightly nutty flavor that's more appealing then ordinary rice.

Melt the butter over medium heat; add the rice and noodles. Cook and stir constantly with a wooden spoon until the rice and noodles become a rich, golden brown.

Serving Suggestion

Terrific with fish, this dish also goes well with meat or poultry.

Vegetable Cheese Tortellini

Prep/Total Time: 15 min.

- 8 cups water
- 1 package (16 ounces) frozen California-blend vegetables, thawed
- 1 package (9 ounces) refrigerated cheese tortellini
- 1/2 cup sharp cheddar cheese spread
- 2 tablespoons milk
- 1/4 teaspoon pepper

In a large saucepan, bring water to a boil. Stir in vegetables and tortellini. Return to a boil; cook for 2-3 minutes or until tortellini is tender.

Meanwhile, in a small saucepan, combine cheese spread, milk and pepper. Cook over low heat until heated through. Drain tortellini mixture and toss with cheese sauce.

Yield: 4 servings.

Kid Appeal

This recipe tastes so good that even kids eat it up and get nutritious vegetables in the process.

Simple Substitutions

The California-blend vegetables can be replaced with any 16-ounce bag of frozen vegetables, such as cauliflower, carrots and pea pods.

For a white sauce, use Swiss cheese spread or refrigerated Alfredo sauce.

Hungarian Salad

Prep/Total Time: 10 min.

1 package (10 ounces) frozen mixed vegetables, thawed
1 cup fresh cauliflowerets
1/4 to 1/2 cup sliced stuffed olives
1/2 cup sliced green onions
1/4 cup vegetable oil
3 tablespoons white vinegar
1 teaspoon garlic salt
1/4 teaspoon pepper

In a bowl, combine the first four ingredients. In a small bowl, whisk together the oil, vinegar, garlic salt and pepper. Pour over vegetable mixture and toss to coat. Serve with a slotted spoon.

Yield: 8 servings.

Cauliflower Facts

One head of cauliflower (about 1-1/2 pounds) yields roughly 3 cups florets.

Use 1 cup in this recipe and the remaining in Beef Chow Mein (p. 60) and Chicken Noodle Stir-Fry (p. 95).

Preparation Pointer

The best way to thaw frozen vegetables is in the microwave. Use the defrost selection, which is about 30% power.

Carrots and Pineapple

Prep/Total Time: 20 min.

2 cups baby carrots
1 can (20 ounces) pineapple chunks
4 teaspoons cornstarch
1/2 teaspoon ground cinnamon
1/2 cup packed brown sugar
1 tablespoon butter

In a saucepan, bring 1 in. of water to a boil; place carrots in a steamer basket over water. Cover and steam for 8-10 minutes or until crisp-tender. Drain pineapple, reserving juice; set pineapple aside.

In a saucepan, combine cornstarch and cinnamon. Add the brown sugar, butter and reserved juice. Bring to a boil; cook and stir for 2 minutes or until thickened. Stir in the carrots and pineapple; heat through.

Yield: 4 servings.

Cute Carrots

The packages of baby carrots found in stores are usually large carrots that have simply been trimmed to smaller lengths.

True baby carrots are pulled from the ground early and look exactly like miniature carrots. You can find them in specialty grocery stores, usually with their green tops still attached.

Apple Spinach Salad

Prep/Total Time: 20 min.

- 1/3 cup mayonnaise
- 4 teaspoons white vinegar
- 4 to 5 teaspoons sugar
- 1/4 teaspoon celery salt
- 1/8 to 1/4 teaspoon pepper
- 4 cups torn fresh spinach
- 1 small unpeeled red apple, sliced

In a small bowl, whisk together the mayonnaise, vinegar, sugar, celery salt and pepper. Let stand for 10 minutes; whisk until sugar is dissolved. In a salad bowl, combine the spinach and apple. Drizzle with dressing and gently toss to coat.

Yield: 4 servings.

Selecting Spinach

Choose spinach with crisp, dark green leaves that aren't limp or damaged.

Wash spinach before storing by removing the stem and rinsing in cold water. Dry thoroughly, then wrap loosely in paper towels. Place in a resealable plastic bag and refrigerate for up to 3 days.

One pound of spinach yields 10 to 12 cups.

Tasty Twist

Replace the apple with fresh raspberries or sliced strawberries.

Dilly Romaine Salad

Prep/Total Time: 10 min.

8 cups torn romaine
1 medium cucumber, sliced
1 cup halved cherry tomatoes
1 small red onion, sliced and separated into rings

CREAMY DILL DRESSING:

1/2 cup evaporated milk
1/2 cup vegetable oil
3 tablespoons cider vinegar
2 teaspoons minced fresh dill
1/2 teaspoon onion salt
1/2 teaspoon dried minced onion
1/2 teaspoon salt
1/2 teaspoon ground mustard
1/8 teaspoon white pepper

In a large salad bowl, toss the romaine, cucumber, tomatoes and onion. In a jar with a tight-fitting lid, combine the dressing ingredients; cover and shake well. Serve with salad. Refrigerate any leftover dressing.

Yield: 12 servings (1 cup salad dressing).

Leaf Lesson

The darker green the lettuce leaves, the more nutritious it is. For example, romaine has seven to eight times as much beta-carotene, two to four times the calcium and twice the amount of potassium as iceberg lettuce.

Preparation Pointer

If you're cooking for a family, cut the romaine, cucumber, tomatoes and onion ingredients in half but make the dressing as is. Refrigerate the dressing for a salad later in the week.

Swiss Onion Crescents

Prep/Total Time: 30 min.

1   tube (8 ounces) refrigerated
    crescent rolls
3   tablespoons shredded
    Swiss cheese, *divided*
2   tablespoons chopped
    green onion
1-1/2 teaspoons Dijon mustard

Unroll crescent dough and separate into
eight triangles. Combine 2 tablespoons
cheese, green onion and mustard; spread
about 1 teaspoon over each triangle.

Roll up from the short side. Place point side down on an ungreased baking sheet and curve into a crescent shape. Sprinkle
with remaining cheese. Bake at 375° for 11-13 minutes or until
golden brown.

Yield: 8 rolls.

Crescents with a Twist

Here's another way to prepare convenient crescent
rolls:

  Do not unroll the cres-
cent dough; cut into eight
equal slices. Place cut side
down on an ungreased bak-
ing sheet. Bake at 375° for
11-13 minutes or until
golden brown.

  Meanwhile, in a small
bowl, combine 2 table-
spoons softened butter, 1/4
teaspoon onion powder and
1/4 teaspoon snipped fresh
dill. Spread over warm rolls
and serve immediately.

Creamy Vegetable Casserole

Prep/Total Time: 30 min.

1 package (16 ounces) frozen broccoli, carrots and cauliflower
1 can (10-3/4 ounces) condensed cream of mushroom soup, undiluted
1 carton (8 ounces) spreadable garden vegetable cream cheese
1/2 to 1 cup seasoned croutons

Prepare vegetables according to package directions; drain and place in a large bowl. Stir in soup and cream cheese. Transfer to a greased 1-qt. baking dish. Sprinkle with croutons. Bake, uncovered, at 375° for 25 minutes or until bubbly.

Yield: 6 servings.

Tasty Substitutions

Get creative when making this casserole! Other vegetable options include cauliflower, carrots and pea pods; Brussels sprouts, cauliflower and carrots; or baby mixed beans and carrots.

If you don't have any cream of mushroom on hand, try condensed cream of celery soup instead.

The garden vegetable cream cheese can be replaced with spreadable chive and onion cream cheese.

Greek Green Beans

Prep/Total Time: 15 min.

1-1/2 pounds fresh green beans, cut
      into 1-1/2-inch pieces
  1 tablespoon olive oil
  1 tablespoon minced fresh garlic
1/4 teaspoon salt
1/2 cup feta *or* mozzarella cheese

In a microwave-safe dish, combine the beans, oil, garlic and salt. Cover and microwave on high for 7-9 minutes or until tender, stirring twice. Stir in cheese.

Editor's Note: This recipe was tested in an 850-watt microwave.

Yield: 5 servings.

Bean Basics

Fresh green beans should be crisp and have a firm, velvety feel. Seeds inside the bean should be small.

Store unwashed beans in a resealable plastic bag and refrigerate for up to 3 days. Before using, wash and snap off the ends.

Serving Suggestion

Nothing beats the flavor of cool and crisp garden-fresh beans. In the heat of summer, eat them raw with French onion dip.

Cheddar Waldorf Salad

Prep/Total Time: 15 min.

 2 large Red Delicious apples, cubed
 2 large Golden Delicious apples, cubed
 1/2 cup chopped pecans
 1/4 cup mayonnaise
 3 tablespoons sugar, *divided*
 1/4 cup chopped fresh *or* frozen cranberries, thawed
 1/4 cup shredded cheddar cheese

In a large bowl, combine the apples and pecans. Combine mayonnaise and 2 tablespoons sugar; add to apple mixture and mix well. Combine cranberries and remaining sugar; sprinkle over apple mixture. Top with cheese.

Yield: 6-8 servings.

Berry Basics

Fresh cranberries should be stored in an airtight container in the refrigerator for up to a month. They can be frozen for 1 year.

A 12-ounce bag yields about 3 cups.

What's in a Name

It's said the Waldorf salad was created at New York's Waldorf-Astoria Hotel in 1896 and originally contained apples, celery and mayonnaise. Over the years, walnuts became a staple ingredient as well.

This tasty version replaces the walnuts with pecans and includes cranberries and cheese.

Zesty Vegetable Skewers

Prep: 10 min. + standing   **Grill:** 10 min.

- 1   garlic clove
- 1   teaspoon salt
- 1/3 cup olive oil
- 3   tablespoons lemon juice
- 1   teaspoon Italian seasoning
- 1/4 teaspoon pepper
- 8   medium fresh mushrooms
- 2   small zucchini, sliced 1/2 inch thick
- 2   small onions, cut into sixths
- 8   cherry tomatoes

In a small bowl, mash garlic with salt to form a paste. Stir in oil, lemon juice, Italian seasoning and pepper.

Thread vegetables alternately onto metal skewers; place in a shallow baking pan. Pour garlic mixture over kabobs; let stand for 15 minutes. Grill for 10-15 minutes, turning frequently, or until vegetables are just tender.

Yield: 4 servings.

Kabob Capers

Unlike wooden skewers, metal skewers don't need to be soaked in water before using. So they're great for busy cooks to have on hand for last-minute grilling.

Be sure to leave some room between the foods on your kabobs so that they cook evenly.

Corn 'n' Pepper Packets

Prep/Total Time: 15 min.

> 4 ears of corn, cut into 2-inch chunks
> 1 medium green pepper, cut into 2-inch strips
> 1 medium sweet red pepper, cut into 2-inch strips
> 2 tablespoons minced fresh parsley
> 3/4 teaspoon garlic salt
> 1/4 teaspoon celery seed
> 1/4 teaspoon pepper
> 1/4 cup butter, melted

In a bowl, combine vegetables, parsley and seasonings. Place on a piece of heavy-duty foil (about 18 in. x 12 in.). Drizzle with butter. Fold foil around vegetables and seal tightly. Grill, covered, over medium-hot heat for 10-12 minutes. Open foil carefully to allow steam to escape.

Yield: 4 servings.

Kernels of Truth

Select corn that has fresh green, tightly closed husks with dry (but not brittle) silk. The stem should be moist, but not chalky, yellow or discolored.

The kernels should be plump and in tight rows up to the tip. They should be firm enough to resist slight pressure.

Keep unshucked ears in opened plastic bags in the crisper drawer and use within 1 day.

Pretty Pear Salad

Prep/Total Time: 15 min.

- 2 cans (one 16 ounces, one 29 ounces) pear halves
- 1 package (8 ounces) cream cheese, softened
- 1 tablespoon sugar
- 1/2 cup seedless grapes, halved

Drain the pear halves, reserving 1 tablespoon of syrup. In a small bowl, beat the cream cheese, sugar and reserved syrup until smooth. Fill pear halves; top with grapes.

Yield: 8 servings.

Cute Idea for Kids

Encourage kids to eat this salad by making puppy dog pear salads!

Spoon the cream cheese filling into 8 mounds on a lettuce-lined plate. Place a pear half upside down over each mound.

Place a prune half on the wide end of each pear for the dog's ear. Place a mandarin orange segment along the bottom for the collar. Place a red maraschino cherry at the narrow end of each pear for the nose. Add a raisin for the eye.

Even families on the go
can indulge in dessert with
this chapter's speedy sweets!

Snickers Cookies
(p. 301)

In-a-Dash Desserts

Lemon Ice
(p. 307)

Chocolate Chip Mousse

Prep/Total Time: 15 min. + cooling

1 cup (6 ounces) semisweet
  chocolate chips
1 package (8 ounces) cream
  cheese, softened
1 teaspoon vanilla extract
1 carton (8 ounces) frozen
  whipped topping, thawed

In a microwave or heavy saucepan, melt chocolate chips; stir until smooth. Cool for 20 minutes.

Meanwhile, in a small mixing bowl, beat cream cheese and vanilla until smooth; beat in melted chocolate. Fold in whipped topping. Spoon into dessert dishes. Refrigerate until serving.

Yield: 4 servings.

Melting Chocolate

When melting chocolate in the microwave, use only microwave-safe containers. Handle the container with a hot pad after heating as the container may be hotter than contents.

Do not overheat because chocolate can scorch easily.

Baking chips may appear formed and unmelted after heating but will lose their shape after stirring.

Cream Puff Pyramids

Prep/Total Time: 15 min.

  2 **cans (21 ounces *each*) cherry pie filling**
 24 **to 32 frozen cream-filled miniature cream puffs, thawed**
  1 **cup (6 ounces) semisweet chocolate chips, melted**
  3 **tablespoons confectioners' sugar**
Whipped cream in a can

In a saucepan, warm cherry pie filling over medium-low heat just until heated through. Place three or four cream puffs on each dessert plate.

Place melted chocolate in a small resealable plastic bag; cut a small hole in a corner of the bag. Spoon about 1/4 cup of warm pie filling over cream puffs; drizzle with chocolate. Dust with confectioners' sugar; garnish with whipped cream.

Editor's Note: This recipe was tested with Delizza frozen cream-filled miniature cram puffs.

Yield: 8 servings.

Preparation Pointer

Be sure to serve these cream puffs right after topping them so they don't become spongy.

Serving Suggestion

When entertaining, set up a dessert buffet with miniature cream puffs, assorted pie fillings, hot fudge sauce, whipped cream and ice cream.

Cranberry Peach Crisp

Prep/Total Time: 30 min.

1   can (15-1/4 ounces) sliced
    peaches, drained
1   can (16 ounces) whole-berry
    cranberry sauce
1/2 cup packed brown sugar
1/2 cup all-purpose flour
1/2 cup crumbled oatmeal *or* sugar
    cookies
1/4 cup chopped walnuts
1/4 cup butter, melted

Arrange peaches in a greased shallow 2-qt. baking dish. Stir cranberry sauce and pour over peaches. Combine brown sugar, flour, cookie crumbs and nuts; sprinkle over fruit. Drizzle with butter. Bake, uncovered, at 400° for 18-20 minutes or until bubbly.

Yield: 4-6 servings.

Preparation Pointer

Save the crumbs from the bottom of the cookie jar to use in this rapid recipe.

Tasty Topping

Consider topping Cranberry Peach Crisp with a dollop of thawed whipped topping or a scoop of vanilla ice cream.

Chocolate Dessert Wraps

Prep/Total Time: 20 min.

> 1/2 cup creamy peanut butter
> 4 flour tortillas (8 inches)
> 1 cup miniature marshmallows
> 1/2 cup miniature semisweet chocolate chips

Vanilla ice cream
Chocolate shavings, optional

Spread 2 tablespoons of peanut butter on each tortilla. Sprinkle 1/4 cup marshmallows and 2 tablespoons chocolate chips on half of each tortilla. Roll up, beginning with the topping side. Wrap each tortilla in heavy-duty foil; seal tightly.

Grill, covered, over low heat for 5-10 minutes or until heated through. Unwrap tortillas and place on dessert plates. Serve with ice cream. Garnish with chocolate shavings if desired.

Editor's Note: Crunchy peanut butter is not recommended for this recipe.

Yield: 4 servings.

Outdoor Dining

When warm weather comes to your area of the country, get out and enjoy it by dining in your backyard.

Grill some burgers and hot dogs and serve with corn on the cob.

While enjoying dinner, pop this dessert on the grill.

Timely Tip

You can assemble these dessert wraps the night before or in the morning; wrap and seal in foil. Refrigerate until ready to use. Just add a few minutes to the grilling time.

Peanut Butter Candies

Prep/Total Time: 30 min.

>   1   package (3 ounces) cream
>   cheese, softened
> 1/4   cup chunky peanut butter
> 1/2   cup confectioners' sugar
> 1/2   cup graham cracker crumbs
> 1/4   cup semisweet chocolate chips
>   1   teaspoon shortening

In a small mixing bowl, beat the cream cheese, peanut butter and confectioners' sugar until blended. Beat in cracker crumbs. Shape into 1-1/2-in. balls. Place on a waxed paper-lined baking sheet.

In a microwave, melt chocolate chips and shortening; stir until smooth. Carefully spoon a small amount of chocolate mixture over each candy. Refrigerate for at least 15 minutes.

Yield: about 1 dozen.

Preparation Pointer

During the week, you're likely pressed for time and can't plan to have the cream cheese softened at room temperature when you're ready to use it.

Instead, remove the cream cheese from the refrigerator and defrost it in the microwave.

Unwrap the cream cheese and place on a microwave-safe plate. Cook at 50% power for about 30 seconds or until you can easily cut a knife through the block. Scrape the cheese off the plate and into a mixing bowl.

Mandarin Berry Cooler

Prep/Total Time: 5 min.

  1 **can (11 ounces) mandarin oranges, drained**
  1 **can (8 ounces) crushed pineapple, drained**
  1 **cup sliced fresh strawberries**
  1 **medium ripe banana, cut into chunks**
  6 **ice cubes**
3/4 **cup milk**

In a blender, combine oranges, pineapple, strawberries and banana; cover and process until blended. Add ice and milk; cover and process until smooth. Serve immediately in chilled glasses.

Yield: 4 servings.

Smoothie Secrets

Add a little more nutrition to your smoothies by stirring in some wheat germ or protein powder.

To grab a smoothie on the go, make them up ahead of time. You can freeze a smoothie and thaw it when needed. Remember to allow space in the container because the smoothie will expand in the freezer.

Angel Food Torte

Prep/Total Time: 10 min.

> 1/2 cup cold milk
> 1 package (3.4 ounces) instant vanilla pudding mix
> 1 can (8 ounces) crushed pineapple, undrained
> 1 carton (8 ounces) frozen whipped topping, thawed
> 1 prepared angel food cake (10 inches)
> 1/2 cup flaked coconut
> Maraschino cherries

In a bowl, combine milk, pudding mix and pineapple; mix well. Fold in the whipped topping. Cut cake horizontally into three layers. Place the bottom layer on a serving plate; spread with 1-1/3 cups pineapple mixture. Repeat.

Place top layer on cake; spread with remaining pineapple mixture. Sprinkle with coconut and garnish with cherries.

Yield: 12 servings.

Preparation Pointer

To cut the cake into three layers, measure the height of the cake; divide the number by three. Mark the height of the bottom layer with a toothpick.

From that toothpick, measure the height of the middle layer and mark it with a toothpick. Measure around the cake, inserting toothpicks every few inches.

Carefully cut each layer above the toothpicks with a serrated knife.

Time-Saving Tip

Or skip the step of cutting the cake into layers and spread the pineapple mixture over the top and on the sides of the cake.

Snickers Cookies

Prep/Total Time: 20 min.

1 tube (18 ounces) refrigerated chocolate chip cookie dough
24 to 30 miniature Snickers candy bars

Cut dough into 1/4-in.-thick slices. Place a candy bar on each slice and wrap dough around it. Place 2 in. apart on ungreased baking sheets. Bake at 350° for 8-10 minutes or until lightly browned. Cool on wire racks.

Yield: 2 to 2-1/2 dozen.

Cookies on a Stick

When you have to cook for a bake sale, make these cookies on a stick!

Insert a lollipop stick into a side of each candy bar until the stick is nearly at the opposite side. Press a cookie dough slice around each candy bar until completely covered. Press dough tightly around the end of the candy bar and stick.

Place 3 in. apart on lightly greased baking sheets. Bake at 350° for 14-16 minutes or until cookies are set. Cool for 1-2 minutes before removing from pans to wire racks to cool.

Raspberry Cupcake Dessert

Prep/Total Time: 10 min.

> 2 cream-filled chocolate cupcakes, cut in half
> 1 to 2 cups heavy whipping cream
> 3 tablespoons confectioners' sugar
> 1/2 teaspoon vanilla extract
> 1 to 1-1/2 cups fresh *or* frozen raspberries, thawed and drained

Additional raspberries, optional

Place one cupcake half each in four dessert dishes. In a mixing bowl, beat cream until soft peaks form. Beat in sugar and vanilla until stiff peaks form. Fold in raspberries. Spoon over cupcakes. Garnish with additional berries if desired. Refrigerate until serving.

Yield: 4 servings.

Preparation Pointer

A 12-ounce bag of whole frozen raspberries is equal to about 3 cups.

Simple Substitution

For even faster preparation, replace the heavy whipping cream with thawed whipped topping. Skip the step of adding the confectioners' and vanilla extract.

Not a fan of chocolate? Use cream-filled sponge cakes instead.

Snack Mix Squares

Prep/Total Time: 30 min.

2-1/2	cups halved pretzel sticks
2	cups Corn Chex
1-1/2	cups M&M's
1/2	cup butter
1/3	cup creamy peanut butter
5	cups miniature marshmallows

In a large bowl, combine pretzels, cereal and M&M's. In a large saucepan over low heat, melt butter and peanut butter. Add marshmallows; cook and stir until marshmallows are melted and mixture is smooth. Pour over pretzel mixture; stir to coat. Press into a greased 13-in. x 9-in. x 2-in. baking pan. Cool until firm; cut into squares.

Yield: about 3 dozen.

Foiled Again

To easily remove the bars from the pan, line the bottom of the pan with foil.

Cut a piece of foil that is larger than the pan. Turn the pan upside down and mold the foil around the bottom and sides of pan. Remove the foil, turn the pan right side up and place the formed foil in the pan, allowing the foil to extend beyond the edges of the pan.

Grease the foil; add mixture. When bars are cool, lift the foil out of the pan.

Puffed Apple Pastries

Prep/Total Time: 25 min.

    1   package (10 ounces) frozen pastry shells
    1   can (21 ounces) apple pie filling
  1/2   teaspoon ground cinnamon
  1/4   teaspoon ground nutmeg

Prepare puff pastry according to package directions. Bake at 400° for 20-25 minutes or until golden brown.

Meanwhile, in a small saucepan, combine the apple pie filling, cinnamon and nutmeg; mix well. Cook and stir over medium-low heat for about 3-4 minutes or until heated through. Remove tops from shells. Fill each with about 1/3 cup of filling. Serve warm.

Yield: 6 servings.

Simple Substitution

Replace the apple pie filling with cherry or blueberry pie filling. Skip the cinnamon and nutmeg.

Timely Tip

Puff pastry shells can be baked and stored in an airtight container for up to 2 days. Before filling, you can reheat them in a 400° oven for 5 minutes.

Microwave Brownies

Prep: 15 min.   **Cook:** 10 min.

  1 **cup sugar**
  2 **eggs**
  1 **teaspoon vanilla extract**
1/2 **teaspoon salt**
1/2 **cup butter, melted**
3/4 **cup all-purpose flour**
1/2 **cup baking cocoa**
  1 **cup chopped walnuts**

In a mixing bowl, beat sugar, eggs, vanilla and salt on medium speed for 1 minute. Add butter; beat until blended. Combine the flour and cocoa. Gradually add to sugar mixture; mix well. Stir in walnuts.

Transfer to a greased microwave-safe 8-in. square dish. Microwave, uncovered, on high for 5-6 minutes, rotating every 2 minutes or until a moist area about 1-1/4 in. in diameter remains in the center (when touched, brownie will cling to your finger while area underneath will be almost dry). Cool on a wire rack. Cut into bars.

Editor's Note: This recipe was tested in an 850-watt microwave.

Yield: 9-12 brownies.

Better Brownies

Don't overmix the batter when making brownies or they'll turn out tough.

It's important to evenly spread the batter in the pan. If one corner is thinner than another, it will cook faster and be over-baked when the rest of the pan is done.

Brownies should cool before they're cut.

Cookie Ice Cream Sandwiches

Prep/Total Time: 15 min.

Peanut butter
- **12** oatmeal raisin cookies
- **1** pint vanilla ice cream

Miniature chocolate chips

Spread peanut butter over the bottom of six cookies. Top with a scoop of ice cream. Top with another cookie; press down gently. Roll sides of ice cream sandwich in chocolate chips. Wrap in plastic wrap. Freeze until serving.

Yield: 6 servings.

Simple Substitutions

Get creative when making this dessert. Use chocolate chip, peanut butter or white chocolate macadamia nut cookies.

Skip the peanut butter and replace the vanilla ice cream with whatever flavor you'd like.

Roll the sandwiches in crushed candy bars or chopped nuts...or skip this step altogether.

Timely Tip

These ice cream sandwiches can be stored in the freezer for weeks, making them a great anytime treat to have on hand.

Lemon Ice

Prep/Total Time: 10 min.

1/4 cup raspberry preserves
2 tablespoons orange juice
1 pint lemon ice *or* sherbet
Chocolate syrup

In a bowl, combine raspberry preserves and orange juice; mix well. Spoon 1 tablespoon each into four dessert dishes. Top each with a scoop of lemon ice. Drizzle with chocolate syrup. Serve immediately.

Yield: 4 servings.

Preserve Pointers

Jam, jelly and preserves are all made from fruit mixed with sugar and pectin. The difference is in the form that the fruit takes.

In jam, the fruit comes in the form of fruit, pulp or crushed fruit. For jelly, the fruit is in fruit juice. The fruit in preserves is in the form of chunks.

Finnish Berry Dessert

Prep/Total Time: 30 min.

1-1/2 cups blueberries
1-1/2 cups fresh strawberries,
       quartered
    1 cup unsweetened raspberries
    3 tablespoons sugar, *divided*
    2 tablespoons cornstarch
1-1/2 cups apple-raspberry juice
Frozen vanilla yogurt, optional

In a large heat-proof bowl, combine fruit and 2 tablespoons sugar. In a saucepan, combine cornstarch and juice until smooth. Bring to a boil; cook and stir for 2 minutes or until thickened. Remove from the heat; cool for 10 minutes.

Pour over fruit; toss to coat. Sprinkle with remaining sugar. Cover and refrigerate until chilled. Serve in individual dessert dishes; top with frozen yogurt if desired.

Yield: 8 servings.

Blueberry Basics

Look for fresh blueberries that are plump, firm and uniform in size. They should have shiny, silver-frosted skins.

Refrigerate the fresh blueberries in a covered container for up to 10 days. Wash and remove stems before using.

One pint is equivalent to about 2 cups.

Easy Rice Pudding

Prep/Total Time: 15 min.

  4   **cups milk**
  1   **package (3 ounces) cook-and-serve vanilla**
       pudding mix
  1   **cup instant rice**
  1   **egg, beaten**
1/4   **teaspoon ground cinnamon**
1/4   **teaspoon vanilla extract**

In a saucepan, combine the first five ingredients; bring to a full boil, stirring constantly. Remove from the heat and stir in vanilla. Cool for 5 minutes, stirring twice. Spoon into individual serving dishes. Serve warm or chill until serving.

Yield: 4 servings.

Simple Substitution

Make this rice pudding with other pudding flavors, like banana cream, coconut cream, French vanilla and lemon.

Stir-In Idea

There are many rice pudding recipe variations. This fast version uses instant rice and pudding mix.

   For more traditional flavor, stir in some raisins or dates.

Quick Crisp Snack Bars

Prep/Total Time: 30 min.

1/2 cup honey
1/2 cup chunky peanut butter
1/2 cup dry milk powder
4 cups crisp rice cereal

In a large saucepan, combine the honey, peanut butter and milk powder. Cook and stir over low heat until blended. Remove from the heat; stir in cereal. Press into an 8-in. square baking dish coated with nonstick cooking spray. Let stand until set. Cut into bars.

Yield: 1 dozen.

Honey Hints

Store honey in an airtight container in a dry place at room temperature for up to a year. When refrigerated, honey crystallizes and forms a gooey, grainy mass.

When measuring honey, lightly oil the measuring cup or spoon first.

Preparation Pointer

To keep the mixture from sticking to your hands as you're pressing it into the pan, first run your hands under cold water, shaking off the excess.

Raspberry Pear Delight

Prep/Total Time: 15 min.

1 **package (10 ounces) frozen sweetened raspberries, thawed**
1 **can (15 ounces) pear halves, drained**
1 **pint raspberry sorbet *or* sherbet**
Hot fudge ice cream topping
Fresh raspberries and mint, optional

In a blender or food processor, puree raspberries; strain seeds. Pour onto four dessert plates. Top with pears and a scoop of sorbet. Drizzle with hot fudge topping. Garnish with fresh berries and mint if desired.

Yield: 4 servings.

Sauce Suggestions

Raspberry sauce is a versatile topping that complements a variety of desserts.

Use it to dress up slices of frozen cheesecake. Or pair it with purchased chocolate brownies or angel food cake.

You can prepare the raspberry sauce in advance. Cover and refrigerate for up to a week.

Toasted Angel Food Cake

Prep/Total Time: 10 min.

  1/4 **cup cream cheese, softened**
    8 **slices angel food cake (3/4 inch thick)**
    4 **to 8 teaspoons raspberry preserves**
    8 **teaspoons butter, softened**
Confectioners' sugar

Spread cream cheese on one slice of cake; spread preserves on second slice. Place slices together, sandwich-style. Spread butter on outsides of cake.

In a skillet over medium heat, toast cake on both sides until lightly browned and cream cheese is melted. Dust with confectioners' sugar.

Yield: 4 servings.

Angel Food Facts

Angel food cake is naturally low in fat by using egg whites. Slices of cake are tasty alone or doctored up in recipes like this.

Store leftover angel food cake in an airtight container at room temperature.

Preparation Pointer

The buttered angel food cake slices can also be broiled or grilled. Broil or grill 4 to 6 inches from the heat source on each side for 1 to 3 minutes or until golden brown.

Quick Caramel Rolls

Prep/Total Time: 30 min.

1/4 **cup butter**
1/2 **cup chopped pecans**
1 **cup caramel ice cream topping**
2 **tubes (8 ounces** *each***)**
refrigerated crescent rolls

Place butter in a 13-in. x 9-in. x 2-in. baking pan; heat in a 375° oven until melted. Sprinkle with pecans. Add ice cream topping and mix well. Remove dough from tubes (do not unroll); cut each section of dough into six rolls.

Arrange rolls in prepared pan with cut side down. Bake at 375° for 20-25 minutes or until golden. Immediately invert onto a serving plate. Serve warm.

Yield: 2 dozen.

Calorie Conscious?

To cut the calories of these rolls, use margarine and reduced-fat crescent rolls.

Serving Suggestion

Surprise your family by making traditional breakfast foods (like bacon and eggs) for dinner some night. As a fast, finger-licking finale, set out a plate of these speedy sweet rolls.

Butterscotch Parfaits

Prep/Total Time: 10 min.

> 2 cups cold milk
> 1 package (3.4 ounces) instant butterscotch pudding mix
> 18 vanilla wafers, coarsely crushed
> 1 carton (8 ounces) frozen whipped topping, thawed
> 6 maraschino cherries, optional

In a mixing bowl, beat milk and pudding mix for 2 minutes or until thickened. In six parfait glasses, alternate layers of pudding, wafer crumbs and whipped topping. Garnish with cherry if desired. Refrigerate until serving.

Yield: 6 servings.

Preparation Pointer

Young kids will get a kick out of crushing the vanilla wafers for this recipe.

Place the cookies in a resealable plastic bag; close bag. Have kids crush cookies slightly with a rolling pin

Serving Suggestion

Instead of making individual Butterscotch Parfaits, you can layer the pudding, wafer crumbs and whipped topping in a clear glass bowl for an easy, yet eye-catching trifle. It's so delicious, even guests will be impressed by this in-a-dash dessert!

Spiced Cookie Strips

Prep/Total Time: 25 min.

- **1** tube (18 ounces) refrigerated sugar cookie dough
- **2** tablespoons all-purpose flour
- **2** tablespoons butter, melted
- **1/2** teaspoon ground nutmeg
- **1/4** teaspoon ground cinnamon
- **1/4** teaspoon ground cloves

Remove cookie dough from package and coat with flour. Shake excess flour onto work surface. Roll out dough on a floured surface into a 12-in. x 8-in. rectangle. Using a pizza cutter or sharp knife, cut rectangle in half lengthwise. Cut widthwise into 1-in. strips. Carefully transfer strips to two ungreased baking sheets.

Combine butter and spices; brush over strips. Bake at 425° for 10-12 minutes or until edges are golden brown. Cool for 2 minutes before removing from pans to wire racks.

Yield: 2 dozen.

Cutout Cookie Capers

When rolling out cookie dough, lightly dust the rolling pin and work surface with flour to prevent sticking.

When making cutout cookies, roll out the dough from the center to the edge, keeping a uniform thickness. If the thickness of the dough is uneven, the cookies will bake unevenly.

Smooth Vanilla Shakes

Prep/Total Time: 5 min.

    2   cups cold milk
    1/3 cup instant vanilla pudding mix
    1   carton (8 ounces) vanilla yogurt
1-1/2   cups vanilla ice cream
    1   small ripe banana

Place all ingredients in a blender. Cover and process until smooth. Pour into chilled glasses. Serve immediately.

Yield: 4 servings.

Flavor Variations

You can vary the flavors in this recipe to suit your family's tastes.

For chocolate lovers, use instant chocolate pudding mix and chocolate ice cream. Or simply switch out the vanilla ice cream with strawberry.

Layered Toffee Cake

Prep/Total Time: 20 min.

2 cups heavy whipping cream
1/2 cup caramel *or* butterscotch ice cream topping
1/2 teaspoon vanilla extract
1 prepared angel food cake (16 ounces)
9 Heath candy bar (1.4 ounces *each*), chopped

In a mixing bowl, beat cream just until it begins to thicken. Gradually add the ice cream topping and vanilla, beating until soft peaks form.

Cut cake horizontally into three layers. Place the bottom layer on a serving plate; spread with 1 cup cream mixture and sprinkle with 1/2 cup candy bar. Repeat. Place top layer on cake; frost top and sides with remaining cream mixture and sprinkle with the remaining candy bar. Store in the refrigerator.

Yield: 12-14 servings.

Preparation Pointer

Use a serrated knife and a sawing motion when cutting angel food cake. If time allows, you may find it helpful to freeze the cake for 30 minutes before slicing.

Tips for Whipping Cream

To successfully whip cream, pour the cold cream into a deep, chilled bowl. Whip on high with a stand or electric hand mixer until soft peaks form.

Strawberry Cookie Tarts

Prep/Total Time: 15 min.

1/2 cup vanilla *or* white chips, melted and slightly cooled
1 package (3 ounces) cream cheese, softened
1/2 cup whipped topping
1/4 cup confectioners' sugar
1 teaspoon lemon juice
1/2 teaspoon vanilla extract
12 sugar cookies (about 2-1/2 inches)
4 to 5 fresh strawberries, sliced

In a small mixing bowl, beat melted chips, cream cheese, whipped topping, sugar, lemon juice and vanilla until smooth. Spread about 1 heaping tablespoon onto each cookie. Top with sliced strawberries. Refrigerate until serving.

Yield: 1 dozen.

Cookie Capers

Pick up a pack of store-bought sugar cookies. Or when you have time, make cookies with refrigerated cookie dough.

Tasty Toppings

Replace the regular frozen whipped topping with a flavored variety such as French vanilla or chocolate.

Instead of using all strawberries, top some tarts with sliced kiwi or mandarin orange segments.

Berry Cream Croissants

Prep/Total Time: 10 min.

4 to 6 croissants
1/2 cup seedless raspberry jam
Whipped cream in a can *or* whipped topping
1-1/4 cups fresh *or* frozen unsweetened raspberries, thawed
Confectioners' sugar, optional

Cut the croissants in half horizontally; spread cut halves with jam. Spread whipped cream over bottom halves; top with raspberries. Replace tops. Dust with confectioners' sugar if desired. Serve immediately.

Yield: 4-6 servings.

Preparation Pointer

Keep a bag of raspberries in the freezer to use in a variety of recipes when fresh berries are hard to come by or are too expensive.

Toned-Down Dessert

If you're watching your waistline and want a smaller dessert, use mini croissants, which you can find in many bakeries.

Chocolate Marshmallow Squares

Prep/Total Time: 15 min.

 8 whole graham crackers (about 5 inches x 2-1/2 inches)
 1 cup miniature marshmallows
1/2 cup semisweet chocolate chips
 2 tablespoons caramel *or* butterscotch ice cream topping

Place whole graham crackers 1 in. apart on a baking sheet. Top each cracker with marshmallows and chocolate chips. Drizzle with ice cream topping.

Bake at 350° for 5-7 minutes or until marshmallows are puffed and chips are slightly melted. Cool for 2-3 minutes before serving.

Yield: 4 servings.

Great Graham Crackers

Cinnamon graham crackers can be used in place of the regular graham crackers in this recipe.

S'more Story

It's believed the Girl Scouts invented the S'more in the 1920s right by the campfire.

After eating one, the young kids supposedly chanted "gimme some more!"

Lemon Cheese Tarts

Prep/Total Time: 20 min.

1 cup prepared lemon pie filling, *divided*

1 package (3 ounces) cream cheese, softened

1/2 cup whipped topping

1/2 cup confectioners' sugar

1 teaspoon lemon juice

1/2 cup fresh raspberries

4 individual graham cracker shells

Additional fresh raspberries, optional

Mint leaves, optional

In a small mixing bowl, combine 3/4 cup pie filling, cream cheese, whipped topping, sugar and lemon juice. Beat until smooth. Place 3-4 raspberries in each shell, pressing down slightly.

Divide cream cheese mixture among the shells. Top with remaining pie filling. Garnish with additional raspberries and mint if desired.

Yield: 4 servings.

Preparation Pointer

Skip the mint garnish for weekday dinners and save it for when entertaining.

Simple Substitution

Lemon and chocolate are perfect partners. So replace the graham cracker shells with chocolate shells. Or look for individual shortbread shells.

Butterscotch Oatmeal Bites

Prep: 10 min.   **Cook:** 10 min. + cooling

2-1/2 cups miniature marshmallows
    1 cup butterscotch chips
  1/4 cup peanut butter
    2 tablespoons butter
    3 cups Cheerios
  1/2 cup raisins
  1/2 cup flaked coconut

In a heavy saucepan, combine the marshmallows, chips, peanut butter and butter. Cook and stir over medium-low heat until chips and marshmallows are melted. Remove from the heat; stir in Cheerios, raisins and coconut. Drop by 1/4 cupfuls onto waxed paper. Let stand for 10 minutes.

Yield: 14-16 cookies.

Butter Is Better

For the best results when baking, use real butter. Margarines with a lower fat content have more water and air and will affect your recipes.

Preparation Pointer

As you're getting dinner ready, have the kids drop the cookie mixture onto waxed paper.

Easy Boston Cream Cake

Prep/Total Time: 25 min.

1-1/2 cups cold half-and-half cream
1 package (3.4 ounces) instant vanilla pudding mix
1 loaf (10-3/4 ounces) frozen pound cake, thawed
3/4 cup confectioners' sugar
2 tablespoons baking cocoa
4 to 5 teaspoons hot water

In a bowl, whisk together cream and pudding mix; let stand for 5 minutes. Split cake into three horizontal layers. Place bottom layer on a serving plate; top with half of the pudding. Repeat layers. Top with third cake layer.

In a small bowl, combine the confectioners' sugar, cocoa and enough water to reach a spreading consistency. Spread over top of cake, letting glaze drizzle down sides.

Yield: 4-6 servings.

A Cake or a Pie?

Colonists would bake their cakes in pie tins, which is likely why the authentic version of this recipe is called Boston Cream Pie.

Dessert in a Dash

Turn a frozen pound cake into speedy strawberry shortcake.

Combine 1 cup sliced strawberries and 1 teaspoon sugar. Spoon onto slices of pound cake. Top with thawed whipping cream.

Microwave Cherry Crisp

Prep/Total Time: 15 min.

 1 can (21 ounces) cherry pie
     filling
 1 teaspoon lemon juice
 1 cup all-purpose flour
 1/4 cup packed brown sugar
 3/4 teaspoon ground cinnamon
 1/4 teaspoon ground allspice
 1/3 cup cold butter
 1/2 cup chopped walnuts
Vanilla ice cream

Combine the pie filling and lemon juice
in an ungreased 1-1/2-qt. microwave-
safe dish; set aside. In a small bowl, combine flour, brown sugar,
cinnamon and allspice; cut in butter until mixture resembles
coarse crumbs. Add walnuts. Sprinkle over filling. Microwave,
uncovered, on high for 5-6 minutes or until bubbly. Serve warm
with ice cream.

Editor's Note: This recipe was tested in a 700-watt microwave.

Yield: 4 servings.

Apple Crisp Idea

For a change of pace, make
apple crisp in the micro-
wave instead.

Place a 21-ounce can of
apple pie filling in an ungreased 1-1/2-qt. micro-
wave-safe dish. Continue
with the recipe as directed.

Preparation Pointer

The easiest way to cut the
cold butter into the flour
mixture is with a food
processor.

Peach Melba Dessert

Prep/Total Time: 15 min.

> 4 individual round sponge cakes *or* shortcakes
> 4 canned peach halves in syrup
> 4 scoops vanilla *or* peach ice cream
> 2 tablespoons raspberry jam
> 1 tablespoon chopped nuts

Place cakes on dessert plates. Drain the peaches, reserving 2 tablespoons syrup; spoon 1-1/2 teaspoons syrup over each cake. Place peach halves, hollow side up, on cakes. Put a scoop of ice cream in each peach. Heat jam; drizzle over ice cream. Sprinkle with nuts. Serve immediately.

Yield: 4 servings.

Speedy Pineapple Dessert

Place four round sponge cakes on dessert plates. Top with a 20-ounce can of drained, crushed pineapple; set aside.

In a bowl, beat 1-1/2 cups cold milk and one package (3.4 ounces) instant vanilla pudding mix until smooth. Fold in 1/2 cup thawed whipped topping; pour over pineapple.

Spread 1-1/2 cups whipped topping over pudding. Sprinkle with 1/2 cup chopped nuts.

Cheesecake Dip

Prep/Total Time: 15 min.

> 4 ounces cream cheese, softened
> 1/3 cup sour cream
> 3 tablespoons confectioners' sugar
> 1 tablespoon milk
> 1/4 teaspoon almond extract
> 1 pint fresh strawberries
> 1/4 cup graham cracker crumbs

In a mixing bowl, beat cream cheese until smooth. Add the sour cream, sugar, milk and extract; mix until smooth. Transfer to a serving bowl. Place the strawberries and crumbs in separate serving bowls. Dip strawberries into cheesecake mixture, then into crumbs.

Yield: about 1 cup.

Strawberry Secrets

Purchase brightly colored berries that are plump and fragrant and that have a fresh green hull attached.

Avoid strawberries with green or white color or those that are mushy or shriveled.

Store strawberries in a shallow container on paper towel in the refrigerator for up to 3 days. Wash just before using.

One pint yields 1-1/2 to 2 cups sliced.

Banana Toffee Cream

Prep/Total Time: 15 min.

1   cup heavy whipping cream,
    whipped
1   cup English toffee bits *or*
    almond brickle chips
2   large ripe bananas, sliced

In a bowl, combine the cream, toffee bits and banana. Spoon into parfait glasses or dishes. Cover and refrigerate until serving.

Yield: 4 servings.

Banana Basics

Unlike other fruits, bananas are picked when green because they continue to ripen.

Look for plump, evenly colored yellow bananas. Some small brown spots indicate ripeness; green tips mean the banana is unripe.

General Recipe Index

This handy index lists every recipe by food category, major ingredient and/or cooking method, so you can easily locate recipes to suit your needs.

Alphabetical
Index